THE EGYPTIANS

CASSELL'S EARLY CULTURE SERIES
Series Editor: Edward R. Sammis

Historical Adviser: Richard A. Fazzini
Assistant Curator of Ancient Art, Brooklyn Museum, Brooklyn, N.Y.

The EGYPTIANS

Pharaohs and Craftsmen

Janet Van Duyn

002480

Illustrated in black and white and full colour

CASSELL · LONDON

CASSELL & COMPANY LTD
35 Red Lion Square, London WC1R 4SG
Sydney, Auckland, Toronto, Johannesburg

First published in Great Britain 1974

ISBN 0 304 29271 0

ACKNOWLEDGMENT
I would like to thank the following people, who gave generously of their time and expert advice toward the preparation of this book: Louise Condit, Junior Museum, Metropolitan Museum of Art; Gail Hathaway, technical adviser to the UNESCO Joint Effort to Save Abu Simbel; Ann Ayres Herrick, Low Heywood School, Stamford, Conn.; Georgia Mansbridge, Sacred Heart College Library, Trumbull, Conn.; Ronald Mansbridge, Cambridge University Press, New York.

J.V.D.

Illustrations secured by McGraw-Hill and Fratelli Fabbri and published pursuant to agreement with Fratelli Fabbri Editori, Milano. Editor, Marie Shaw; Art and Design, James K. Davis, Barbara Asch

Printed in Italy by Fratelli Fabbri Editori, Milano, and bound in Great Britain

F 673

Contents

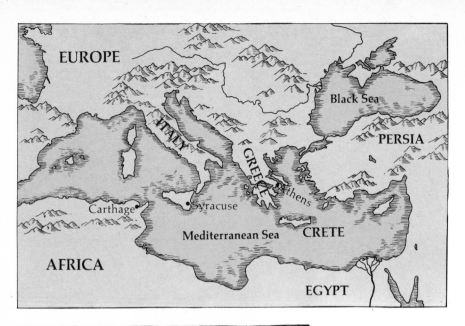

The Mediterranean
World of which
Egypt was a part
(above) and the
Kingdom of Egypt
along the Nile
about 1500 B. C.
(below).

Introduction

EVER since the Greeks first visited Egypt centuries ago, the land has been looked upon as the great antiquity among civilizations. Egypt also holds fascination as a land of mystery; of strange hieroglyphs; of gods with animal heads; of multi-colored sarcophagi; of elaborately embalmed mummies; of gigantic pyramids.

In addition there is about Egypt an aura of timelessness. It has traditionally been considered the eternal land where things never changed; the sun rose and set visibly every day; the Nile's flooding fertilized the land each spring; the people followed the cycles of life, all the while building the tombs in which they could continue that life forever.

This concept is strengthened by visits to a museum where, to the average beholder, all Egyptian art appears to look alike. It is indeed true that there are elements common to the art of all periods. It is true as well that many aspects of religion, government, and daily life changed little throughout the course of history. The Egyptians, in a sense, always wanted to maintain the past in the present.   Egyptian kings were fond of comparing their achievements with those of bygone kings. Priests pored through ancient documents for solutions to current spiritual problems.   Artists and sculptors were often influenced, both as to subject matter and style, by earlier works of art.

Egyptian culture, however, spanning many centuries and conditions of drastic change, can hardly be looked upon as static.   To see that this is so, we only need to contrast a ruler of the earlier period with one of a later era.   The former would have been a true god-king, looked upon with awe, an absolute monarch holding sway in relative isolation from the rest of the world.   The latter, for various reasons, would no longer be looked upon as the god his predecessor was.   He had become a great warrior ruling over a polyglot empire embracing many peoples and many tongues.   The earlier king, in his isolation from the world outside, was secure, self-satisfied, and somewhat limited in his outlook.   His universe was Egypt.

The acquisition of empire, bringing with it increased contact with the world outside, also brought wealth, new ideas, and an appetite for the ornate and the elegant.   The carvings on the tombs of these periods show elaborate banquets, complete with musicians and dancing girls; they show long lines of subject peoples bringing tribute.   Both life and the afterlife had become infinitely more complex and more sophisticated.

Having established that change did take place in the development of the nation, it is nevertheless possible to make a few statements about the ancient Egyptian which are generally applicable and true.

One of his most striking characteristics was his optimism, his confidence in himself, in his god-king and in the existence of a hereafter.   Because of the inordinate amount of time he spent in building his tomb, he may have given the impression that he was preoccupied with death; on the contrary it was a way of saying that his love for life was so great that he wished to prolong it beyond the grave. If his palaces, which were made of less durable stuff, had been as well preserved, our picture of him would have been in better balance.

The Egyptian was a devoutly religious man. His gods to him were very real and important. They ruled the universe and their well-being was necessary both to his own well-being and that of his country. The gods, like himself, needed homes, food and clothing; hence the large number of temples (god-houses) where the statues in which the gods manifested themselves were clothed and fed.

People did not intercede personally with their gods, at least in the formal state religion—the religion of the royalty and upper classes. Only their king, a god himself, was worthy to do that. It is the king only whom we find depicted on the temple walls in the act of making an offering to the deities. Little is known of the religious beliefs and practices of the common people.

The Egyptian was a man who felt at home with his gods, with his government, with society and with nature. The universe—both the gods' and man's—functioned according to a universal order. That order was known as Ma'at. It was man's first duty to live by Ma'at. To transgress was to bring chaos, which was evil. To follow it was to maintain order, which was good.

Richard A. Fazzini

Assistant Curator of Ancient Art
Brooklyn Museum, Brooklyn, N.Y.

Funeral statue in cedar wood and bronze was found in Tutankhamon's
tomb. Museum of Cairo.

chapter 1

TREASURES OF TUTANKHAMON

"Infinite riches, in a little room."

Christopher Marlowe, *The Jew of Malta*.

ON November 6, 1922, Lord Carnarvon, financier of many excavations in Egypt, received a cable at his home in England. It was from Howard Carter, his associate in Egypt, who was digging in the Valley of the Kings, a burial ground for pharaohs near Thebes. For years archaeologists had dug the Valley, almost literally leaving no stone unturned. All that remained untouched was a small triangle of rubble-filled land. It looked highly unpromising, but Carter had insisted on exploring further, just to assure himself that there was nothing more to find.

The cablegram read: "At last have made wonderful discovery in Valley; a magnificent tomb with seals intact; recovered same for your arrival; congratulations. Carter."

Carnarvon left England at once for Luxor. Visiting the site, he agreed that the debris-filled flight of steps Carter had found might well lead to the tomb of Tutankhamon, a pharaoh known only by name from the old king lists and from artifacts picked up in the vicinity.

They set a crew of men to work clearing the stairway as far

Sculptured wood throne chair covered with gold and embellished with multi-colored glass, stone and silver, was one of many treasures in Tutankhamon's tomb. Museum of Cairo.

as the door Carter had seen.   But to their great disappointment they found that the seals were not intact; they had been broken, then carefully resealed.   Nevertheless they pressed on through a passage to a second door bearing the seal of Tutankhamon. Again—clear evidence of someone having broken in, perhaps twice.

Grave robbers had been there, without a doubt.   Would the archaeologists find this tomb, like so many others, ruthlessly plundered?

Carter, an experienced digger and engineer, and probably one of the most patient men on record, knew better than to rush things.   Too often eager amateurs in the past had destroyed evidence before they had realized its worth.   Carefully he cut a small hole in the top of the door, just large enough for him to pass his hand through.   Then he lit a candle, inserted it in the opening and peered inside.   Behind him, a small group of tense watchers awaited his verdict.

At first Carter could see nothing.   The candle flickered in the stifling atmosphere, but did not go out.   Then, as Carter's eyes grew accustomed to the darkness, the faint, wavering light seemed to pick up glints of gold here and there—animal faces, statues, shapes.

For a moment he couldn't speak.   In his own words, he was "struck dumb."

Carnarvon's impatient voice prodded him.   "Can you see anything?"

"Yes," Carter replied, "wonderful things!"

The large antechamber behind the door proved to be a storehouse of incredibly magnificent furnishings.   Once they got in they could see chests, vases, gold stools, chairs—rich appointments of a king whose sepulcher was surely nearby.   They found the place in wild disorder, rather like an attic in which someone had piled up the family furniture.   At the far end of the chamber, two striking black and gold statues holding gold wands stood in front of another door bearing royal seals.

Again Carter had to restrain his eagerness. Haste would be fatal. He insisted that his men list and store every single object in the antechamber before trying to find out what lay beyond the door. This meant organizing a team of photographers, draftsmen, language experts, archaeologists.

The most striking objects in the antechamber were three gold-plated couches, ornamented with the heads of three animals: a lioness, a hippopotamus, and a cow. Under one of the couches was the king's throne, truly magnificent with its glass inlay and semiprecious stones. On the backrest was a picture of Tutankhamon himself against a background of gold. He was sitting on his throne, his wife standing just in front. Over their heads shone the sun's disk with downward rays, symbol of the god Aton.

As they cleared the antechamber the explorers discovered behind one of the couches still another door. Someone had made a small hole and crawled through. Peering inside, Carter and his companions saw that this room was a smaller repository of objects. It had not been robbed. They named it the Annex and decided to leave it sealed until the very last.

After weeks of painstaking work the antechamber was cleared and its contents faithfully documented. The workers found one large chest open, its garments spilling over on the floor. A handful of gold rings tied up in a handkerchief had obviously been dropped in someone's effort to get out fast. A gang of thieves at some time had apparently started to rob the tomb but they had been interrupted in the middle of the job. Perhaps priests had discovered the plunderers and chased them out, after which they had tidied up as quickly as they could, relocking the doors.

Now it was time to tackle the Annex. Once more Carter chipped away a small hole at the top, just under the lintel, and flashed an electric torch through the opening.

This time there were no faint glimmerings in the dark. Carter found himself facing a wall of solid gold. It seemed

to block the entrance to the chamber.   For once, the robbers had been thwarted.

The "wall" proved to be an immense shrine built around the king's coffin.   Inside was another, and another, and another—seven coffins in all—like a nest of boxes.   They were wedged against one another so tightly that there was barely space to pass a finger between them.

Thanks to Carter's patience and engineering skill, the men managed to lift each coffin out without damaging the rich ornamentation.   The four outer coverings were heavy and rectangular in shape; the three inner ones had the anthropoid ("mummy") shape of Egyptian sarcophagi.   After months of work the men found themselves looking at King Tutankhamon himself—the only Egyptian pharaoh ever to be found, to date, his riches almost intact, inside his own sarcophagus and tomb.

A mask of gold had been placed over the mummy, reaching

(Left top.)   Masks of gold from Tutankhamon's tomb.   (Left bottom.) Headboard from a bed found in the royal tomb, representing the god of eternity kneeling under the gold sun symbol.   (Above.)   The work of talented Egyptian artisans is reflected in this painted wood coffin, part of the Tutankhamon treasure.   All in the Museum of Cairo.

to the knees. The features of the young king were sharply molded; his arms were crossed, bearing the flail and scepter.

The delicate task of unwrapping the yards of linen fell to Dr. Douglas Derry, English surgeon and anatomist. As he carefully unwound each strip, he came upon jewels and precious objects imbedded in the cloth. Even the fingers and toes of the pharaoh were bedecked with golden coverings, like false nails. Most touching of all was a small wreath of real flowers, their colors faint but still discernible, which someone close to the king (a wife, or a child?) had laid on his forehead.

In view of all this opulence the body of the king seemed small and pathetic. Nevertheless Dr. Derry was able to determine that Tutankhamon was in his late teens when he died.

Who was this boy-king? A relatively unimportant pharaoh, he lived about 1358 B.C. He was the son-in-law of Akhenaton, famous heretic ruler in the Eighteenth Dynasty, who tried to promote belief in one god. Tutankhamon probably came to the throne when he was twelve, and could not have reigned for more than seven years. From objects in the tomb we know that his interests were those of other boys. There were bows and arrows, games which resembled chess, darts, and throw-sticks—one was labeled "made by the king's own hand."

How did he die? Nobody knows. Some people are convinced that he was murdered and his body hustled off into a tomb which may have been intended for someone else. It was too small to hold the sumptuous ornaments crowded into it, and it was certainly much smaller than many of the tombs of other Egyptian kings. But all this is conjecture, not fact.

Tutankhamon lived during a turbulent period in Egypt's history. Undoubtedly he was manipulated by his advisers who wished to rise to power themselves. In view of the conflicting

Dagger inlaid with gold. British Museum.

desires of the people surrounding him, this boy in his teens could not have been a very forceful king.

Insignificant as he was, he was obviously given one of the most magnificent funerals in history, bringing to mind Shakespeare's ironic words:

> ... nothing in his life
> Became him like the leaving of it.

There is more to the story of the excavation and it is not all happy. The Egyptian government made things difficult by refusing to curb the hordes of sightseers who came swarming to the spot, crowding into the tomb, seriously hampering the work of the archaeologists. Carter was short-tempered when it came to dealing with bureaucrats and financiers. Incurring the wrath of the government, he closed all operations and went back to England.

Fortunately the tomb was kept under surveillance by Carter's loyal coworkers. A letter from one of them, Ruis Ahmed Gurgar, assures him that everything is "alright," and ends "Longing to your early coming."

Carter did return, and order was eventually restored. The Cairo Museum received its treasure, along with Tutankhamon's sarcophagus and gold mask. The mummy was replaced in the second inner coffin and put back in the tomb, where it lies today.

The tidal wave of publicity was to reach considerable proportions before it died down. Tourists continued to invade Egypt, armed with cameras and notebooks. The archaeologists were deluged with letters—praising, condemning, asking questions, making suggestions. Sellers of fake antiquities foisted "treasures" on the gullible. Someone revived the old myth of mummy wheat (long since proved false), that seeds locked in the tomb for 4,000 years would sprout if planted.

Headlines everywhere blazed with the story of "King Tut." In America King Tut clothing styles and a King Tut popular song occupied people's minds. *The Egyptian Scarab Mystery,* by S. S. Van Dine, was a popular thriller.

The sudden death of Lord Carnarvon in 1923 didn't exactly calm the thrill-seekers. Although he died from perfectly natural causes—pneumonia which followed the bite of a virulent mosquito—the press began dropping dark hints about a poisonous scarab beetle in the tomb. Thus was born the legend of the "pharaoh's curse," whose gripping power was every bit as good as the Saturday afternoon movies. In the following months twenty other persons who died, some having a faint connection with the tomb excavators, were proclaimed as "victims" in banner headlines.

It was fun while it lasted—then the furor died down. Twenty-six years later, Dr. Derry, the surgeon, drily remarked, "As one who actually unwrapped the mummy of the king, the supposed curse should rest most heavily on me and I should have been the first to die." He lived well into his eighties.

What did the discovery of King Tutankhamon's tomb really prove to the world? His name will go down in history as the first Egyptian pharaoh to be found in his final resting place, surrounded by the objects he loved in life. Other discoveries of tomb treasures would follow, but none would have the excitement, or the completeness, of this one. One noteworthy fact is the presence of an iron dagger in the tomb—one of the first iron objects ever to turn up in Egypt.[1]

Directions buried with Tutankhamon read thus: "Thou goest forth out as a god, going out as Atum, O Osiris, Tutankhamon. . . ." This sent him on his long journey to the afterlife. And surely the benevolent spirit, which the Egyptians call the Ka, watched over his earthly remains in its seven coffins, one inside the other, so that unborn generations could hear his story.

[1] Tutankhamon's tomb and treasure were significant for many reasons. First, it aroused international interest in Egypt and Egyptology. Because the tomb had not been plundered, its contents provide us with our best evidence about the nature of a royal burial and certain aspects of Egyptian funerary practices. Second, the treasure gives us information about the art of the period; while the foreign stylistic features exhibited by many objects show something about the international relations at that time.

chapter 2

THE GIFT OF THE NILE

"All day we follow the sacred course of the river
Between the mud villages of the living
And the stone-hewn tombs of the dead."

Elizabeth Coatsworth, *The Nile.*

W HEN the Greek historian
Herodotus visited Egypt in 470 B.C., he marveled at the well-ordered, cultivated land along the banks of the Nile. He called it "the gift of the river." Almost completely surrounded by desert, the people who lived there had the two essentials for survival—food and water. In the dark alluvial soil crops flourished; Egyptians called this the Black Land. Beyond lay the barren, rocky desert, or Red Land.

Everywhere Herodotus went he took notes. "All the country which the Nile waters is Egypt," someone told him, "and all those are Egyptians who dwell below the city Elephantine, and drink of that river."

Not quite. In those days no one had the remotest idea of the extent of the African continent. Nor did anyone dream

22

A woman carrying fruit and bread dominates this relief. Note pictographic writing on the bottom.

(Left.) Bull plaque from the time of King Narmer. Louvre. (Above.) The model of an Egyptian boat.

that the Nile was 4,000 miles long and that one of its sources (not to be discovered until 1857) lay in Lake Victoria far to the south.   But Herodotus was right in assuming that the Egyptians, for the most part, lived "below the city Elephantine," on an island just above the First Cataract.   To the south of it began a series of six cataracts or rapids, which kept the river from being navigable.   The ancient Egyptians never got much farther than the Fourth Cataract in Nubia (now Sudan) during their exploration of the river.

From Aswan the Nile flows tranquilly in a northerly direction until it reaches the Mediterranean.   About sixty miles before it gets there it breaks up into a complex of rivers and canals, covering a region called the Delta because of its triangular shape.   The flat, marshy region differs from the land to the south, where the river—and its adjacent lands—stretches like a thin green oasis into the desert.

Slate tablet called "The Narmer Palette" shows the king preparing to strike a prisoner with a mace. Museum of Cairo.

In ancient times the two kingdoms of Lower and Upper Egypt were separate. We have little to tell us about this period except legends and a few artifacts. One of the oldest objects in good state of preservation is a flat, engraved stone, about the size and shape of a small artist's palette. It shows the king, Menes (or Narmer), wearing the crowns of both the North and South while subjugating a king of the Upper Kingdom. Menes may have been a king named Narmer or Hor-aha, or even a legendary combination of several different kings, all of whom contributed to the uniting of the Upper and Lower Kingdoms.

The Narmer Palette, as it is called, tells us in effect that this ruler worked at uniting these two kingdoms. Menes is thought to be the founder of the capital, Memphis, which was created at the base of the Delta. Like Washington, D.C., Egypt's first capital was strategically placed midpoint between the North and the South.

Using the Nile as a main artery, Menes found it easy to communicate with all parts of his kingdom. There were no mountain barriers, no desert wastes to cross, no dense forests to penetrate. Light river boats, at first made of tightly bound reeds, and later sometimes made of wood, could be poled north with the current. Going upstream, the Egyptians used oars. Sails were also used to pick up the prevailing north wind. Thus from very early days the Nile played a key role in uniting the country.

But the Nile's most unusual feature was, and is, its annual flood, which is unlike that of any other river in the world. When the Mississippi overflows its banks it can often bring disaster, because it crests without warning, usually after an unusually heavy spring thaw. The Nile flood is dramatic, but predictable. Every year an accumulation of water from the spring monsoons in Ethiopia comes rushing in torrents through the country's deep gorges. By early summer the waters of the Nile begin to rise and spread slowly over the land. When they subside in the fall they leave behind a rich deposit of fertile silt. The overflow may vary in volume from year to year. There may be periods of poor crops and famine, but more often Egyptian farmers report good years and abundant crops.

The flood has always been so dependable Egyptians learned to live by it. Very early they mastered the tricks of keeping high and dry; for one thing, they built their villages on mounds, just out of range of the spreading water. Later on, in the Pyramid Age, they situated their huge construction works at the very edge of the desert, near enough to the river for boats to float materials to the site, far enough away to keep the works from being inundated.

Early Egyptians, like people of all developing civilizations, noticed a regularity to the seasons. They could clock their seasons with their flood. In the spring, the Nile began to rise. The time between the risings, the Egyptians found, was approximately 365 days, if it was averaged out. Thus they evolved their calendar, with its three "agricultural" seasons, which is essentially the same as the calendar we use today.

Not knowing that the year was actually a little longer than 365 days, they never thought of leap year. They divided their 365-day year into twelve months of thirty days. At the end of the year they added five festival days. The omission of leap year finally brought their calendar seasons out of step with the real seasons.

The harvest is underway in this tomb relief.

Fishermen pull in their nets brimming with fish. Note that aquatic birds decorate the center panel of this tomb relief.

Months had three periods of ten days each. Grouped in fours, they made up the three seasons: Inundation; Winter; Summer. Day and night were divided into twenty-four hour segments; but the hours were not of equal length. In the summer the daylight hours were long and the night hours short. In the winter the ratio was reversed.

This ancient form of daylight saving was a real boon to hard-working, thrifty Egyptians. Very early they learned to make the most of their resources, one of which was light. They did this as much for work as for pleasure.

Their greatest problem was how to save water. First attempts to control the Nile apparently took the form of long ditches leading to basins, or big pools. Ditches grew into canals as farmers, and later on, engineers, tested irrigation methods. A vast irrigation project in a marshy section called Fayum gave Egypt one of her first large-scale reservoirs. Today Egypt is assured a water supply all year round by a complete network of canals, reservoirs, and dams.

Egyptians, for the most part, were not inventors or innovators. But they had the knack of discovering a simple principle and making it work to their advantage. To convey water out of the river and into their gardens they used a device called a *shadoof* in Arabic—a long pole with a bucket on one end and a heavy weight on the other. It was balanced on a forked support, seesaw style. When the farmer wanted to water his garden he simply set up the shadoof on the bank of the river, lowered the bucket, swiveled the forked support, swung the bucket out over to the land to be watered, and dumped it. This simple arrangement may still be seen in country areas today.

With a controlled water supply the Egyptians found that they could produce two sets of crops a year. Also, as we know from pictures in tombs and temples, the river abounded in fish, and game inhabited the marshlands.

The river was always busy. Boats ferried people, animals, goods from place to place. Protected by her deserts and cataracts, Egypt had little to fear from invaders. She lived peace-fully, for the most part, so well-satisfied, so disciplined in her living habits, her customs, her business affairs, her art, and her manner of dress, that she changed surprisingly little in two thousand years.

Two remarkable plants grew in abundance along the Nile, the papyrus and the lotus. Each was to contribute to making Egypt famous. The first gives its name to paper, which the Egyptians invented by pounding the fibrous pith into smooth sheets. This tough plant grew in the impenetrable thickets of the Delta, its stems sometimes reaching a height of nineteen feet. Parts of it were useful for making ropes, sails, skiffs, baskets—and even articles of clothing, sandals or loincloths. Tightly bound together, the tough stems made columns, which set the style for papyroform columns at Karnak.

To the aesthetic Egyptians the fragrant lotus, or water lily, floating serenely on the surface of quiet pools to the south, was pure beauty. The blossoms, some white, some blue, opening in the morning and closing at night, suggested the rhythm of life.

The lotus flower had another, deeper meaning. The Egyp-tians believed that the lotus was the cradle of the sun on the first morning. It symbolized the emergence of life out of the watery Chaos which existed before the universe was born.

These symbols of the useful and the beautiful portrayed the two aspects of Egyptian life. The papyrus showed the stern practicality of her mind; the lotus, the delicacy of her spirit. But there was another aspect important in Egyptian life. Something caused the lotus and papyrus to grow. Something caused the seasons to change, light to come, crops to flourish. As the early Egyptian stood looking at a small seed in his hand, knowing that when he put it in the ground some mysterious change would take place causing it to spring forth and bear fruit, he had but one thought: Who or what makes it happen? After some 5,000 years, we are still asking that question.

Osiris, god of the dead, could cause seed to spring from the ground. He became the god of all growing things—fruit, grain, and especially wheat. In the very old days people used to put wheat-stuffed figures, called effigies, of Osiris in tombs. When the seed sprouted, suggesting rebirth, Osiris came to preside over the dead, promising a safe journey to the afterlife.

Osiris himself was said to have risen from the dead in a highly miraculous manner. It happened in this way: One of his seventy-two brothers, Set, a boisterous fellow, built a coffin and jokingly told his brother to get inside to see if it was the right length. When Osiris climbed in, Set snapped the lid shut, sealed it, and threw the coffin into the Nile.

Osiris' wife, Isis, was beside herself with grief and rage. She retrieved the coffin, but the wily Set got at the body and, as the story goes, "rent it in fourteen pieces." Sorrowfully Isis put her dismembered husband back together again, binding him carefully with long linen bandages. Gently she fanned the breath of life in him. He then became king of the afterworld, presiding in his full regalia of bandages—the prototype of the Egyptian mummy.

Vengeance was to come. A short time afterward, Horus, son of Isis and Osiris, killed Set. He became one of Egypt's protectors, a god's son come to earth to champion mankind.

After Upper and Lower Egypt were united under Menes the country entered into her first great period of prosperity, under the Old Kingdom, which archaeologists date as beginning somewhere between 3100 B.C. and 2800 B.C. The people looked on their king, or pharaoh, as a deity. They represented him in huge, larger-than-life statues and followed his leadership without question. Even the title of pharaoh, which is represented by the Egyptian hieroglyph *per-o,* or large house, suggests the enormous dignity of the king. Actually the title was not in common use until many centuries later, but historians have applied it to all of the three kingdoms. It has a certain aptness for these Egyptian god-kings, who were like no others.

A joyous hunting scene, in delicate color, from about 1500 B.C., has
miraculously survived. British Museum.

chapter **3**

WHO WERE THE EGYPTIANS?

A trick spoon which probably belonged to an elegant Egyptian.   Louvre.

"Concerning Egypt itself I shall extend my remarks to a great length, because there is no country that possesses so many wonders, nor any which has such a number of works which defy description."

Herodotus, *Persian Wars*, Book II.

IN the family hunting expedition in the papyrus swamp everyone seems to be having a good time.   The man is preparing to bring down waterfowl with a throw-stick.   Just behind him, his wife is holding a sheaf of reeds, while his daughter kneels at his feet, gathering lotus blossoms.   They have taken their reed skiff for an outing, bringing the family cat for a retriever.   There is also a goose in the picture, apparently not hunted, but himself hunting—is he another family pet?   Butterflies, herons, and fish complete the picture of a lovely day and a happy family on a picnic.

Families in ancient Egypt were much like our own.   An Egyptian child could enjoy real companionship with his parents. Unlike the pharaohs, who supported harems and married relatives to insure the royal line, a common man could usually afford one wife only.   It was a plain matter of economics.

Polygamy was for the rich. As the head of the household, he honored the woman who ran it and who brought up the children. A woman could go about as she pleased; she was in no way repressed by society or enslaved by her household duties. "Multiply the bread that you give your mother," a son was instructed. "Carry her as she carried you."[1]

As we can see in the picture, the Egyptian mode of dress was plain: a short, kilted white linen skirt for men, a longer, clinging white linen garment for women. These uncomplicated styles varied little for 2,000 years; their simple lines set off admirably the jeweled collars and bracelets that show up in paintings.[2] The Egyptians became highly skilled goldsmiths, metal workers, and jewelers.

The pendant shown in the illustration, now in the Metropolitan Museum of Art in New York, is one of the most beautiful pieces of jewelry ever found in Egypt. The two falcons face each other; sun disks are over their heads. This beautifully balanced design is composed of 372 pieces of lapis lazuli, turquoise, carnelian, and garnet. It was a gift of Sesostris II of the Twelfth Dynasty to his daughter.

Women had an obsessive concern for their hair, just as they do today. Straight, dark, carefully trimmed locks reached their shoulders, or hung farther down their backs.[3] (Men wore theirs shorter, sometimes completely shaved off. They, as a rule, had no beards, as did the men of Asia Minor. The king wore a false and symbolic beard often in artistic works.)

---

[1] Men were, as they still are, freer than women. In only a few exceptional cases did women rule Egypt, and almost all scholars, craftsmen, government officials, and clergy were men. The scribes were men. Most women found their place in the home. This does not mean, however, that they were not honored.

[2] While the simple kilt for men and the lengthy clinging dress for women enjoyed an incredibly long usage, to judge by the representations in tombs and temples, styles went through cycles. The Egyptians took great pride in their appearance, a fact that might seem contradicted by their simple dress, which was made necessary, however, by the warm climate.

[3] The long hair seen on women in sculpture and painting is more often a representation of a wig than real hair. Men did not usually wear beards, but there were numerous exceptions to this rule.

For formal occasions a woman often wore a wig or a headdress. In many paintings, especially those of banquets, we see odd-looking cones on top of a woman's (and occasionally a man's) head. Made of sweet-smelling wax, they melted near the body heat, thus adding to the allure of the wearer. Nobody seemed to mind the stickiness.

Little children conveniently wore no clothes at all. Boys wore a long twist of hair over the right temple. This curious squiggle, like a question mark, found its way into the written language as the hieroglyph for *child*.

Egyptian children loved to play. Many tomb pictures show the whole family participating. A boy might play a nightly game of *zenet* with his father, using a board with counters, like checkers. With his friends he could play the serpent game,

(Left.) Ornate necklace was worn by a princess. The Metropolitan Museum of Art. Contribution from Henry Walters and the Rogers Fund, 1916. (Center.) Bes was the homely household god. Museum of Cairo. (Right.) Carved from wood, this toy contains moveable parts. British Museum.

like parcheesi, or the goose game, following the pattern of pursuit and capture as so many of our games do today.

As for sports, there was always the ball. Girls played catch, but usually with each other, in the family garden. For the very young there were dolls, rattles, tops, and some mechanical toys. The surprisingly accurate pictures of two wrestlers, which cover the walls of the chapel of Beket at Beni Hasan, show the Egyptian attitude toward strenuous sport. They were aesthetic, as well as competitive.[1]

The walled garden, with its pool (not for swimming, but for beauty), its flowers and vegetables, its sycamore trees, must have been a pleasant gathering spot. Here children could play, dogs could bark, cats could prowl, while parents sat in the shade of the pillared porch. The house, just behind, was of simple design. Built of river clay or brick, it often had a straw roof so that the smoke of cooking fires could pass through. In a hot, sunny climate a family needed very little protection from the elements; the main problem was to keep cool. People slept on straw mats or low cots. Tables, chairs, and other articles of furniture usually followed spare, clean lines with few changes in their designs through the years.

[1] The Egyptians, judging from the evidence we have, were quite competitive as individuals. They were proud of their achievements, often to the point of boasting.

RISE OF EGYPT'S EMPIRE

DATES	PEOPLE TO REMEMBER	THINGS TO REMEMBER
Before 3000 B.C.		Stone Age People. Artifacts found near El Badari
After 3000 B.C. Dyn. I-II	Menes (Narmer)	God-King Uniter of Upper and Lower Egypt.
After 2780 B.C. Dyn. III-VI Old Kingdom	Zoser Imhotep Khufu (Cheops) Khafre (Chephren) Menkaure (Mycerinus)	"Step Pyramid" evolved from Mastaba tombs. "The Wise" Architect, Scribe, Healer, later deified. Great Pyramid Sphinx PYRAMID AGE CAPITAL-MEMPHIS
After 2100 B.C. Dyn. VII-X-XI		Chaos. Weak Pharaohs Prowling Libyans and Semites.
After 2000 B.C. Dyn. XII-XV Middle Kingdom	Amenemhet I Amenemhet III	Expansion. Trade to Crete, Syria. Annexation of Nubia. Flowering of Literature and Arts. Ma'at CAPITAL-THEBES Colossal statues..."Labyrinth."
After 1785 B.C. Dyn. XVI-XVII	Kamose	Hyksos. "Shepherd Kings". Introduction of horse and chariot.
After 1580 B.C. Dyn. XVII-XX New Kingdom	Ahmose Hatshepsut Senmut Thutmose III Amenhotep III Akhenaton Nefertiti Tutankhamon Ramses II Merneptah Ramses III-XI	Rout of Hyksos. Woman-Pharaoh. Voyage to Punt. Architect. Temple of Hatshepsut. 20 military expeditions. Battle of Megiddo. EGYPTIAN EMPIRE NOW AT ITS HEIGHT. THEBES. AMON Amarna interlude. Aton-One God Famed for her beauty. First Pharaoh to be found intact in tomb in 1923. Called "The Great." Extravaganza. Battle of Kadesh. Probable exodus of Hebrews. Invasions. "People from the Sea." Slow decline under Ramessid kings.

Bes, a grotesque, dwarfish little household god, was special protector of the home. He was supposed to keep men from "evil influences," reptiles, and other harmful creatures. He watched over women, especially in childbirth. His happy, reassuring grin seems to tell us that he will cheerfully clean up messes, chide naughty children, and chase away pesky intruders. He is reminiscent of the brownie in Celtic folklore, who kept the house free from blight and disorder. At any rate, this ugliest of Egyptian gods must certainly have boosted a family's morale by reminding them to laugh.

Who were the Egyptians? Where did they come from? What were they like? In prehistoric times they undoubtedly drifted off the desert in search of water. The Nile, with its flooding banks, promised yearly replenishment of a scarce commodity. In its prehistoric period, we have a sequence of cultures that can be termed Egyptian. But it was not until Dynasty I that these people created what we can call a civilization. The rise of this civilization seems to be at least partly inspired by contacts with more advanced Near Eastern peoples.

From the few pieces of evidence found so far, it would appear that the early Egyptian was lithe, slight of build, and long-legged. His hair was jet black, his skin deep tan. He must have admired physical fitness or cultivated it; there are relatively few paintings of grossly fat Egyptians.

In the paintings, which appear so much alike, we can see definite character traits if we look closely. Cheerful, tranquil faces look back at us. The Egyptian rarely has an expression of arrogance. Rather, his dignity is much in evidence. Even a proud pharaoh has a quality of poise. Like the working man, he is intent on what he is doing.

The Egyptians were probably the most industrious people the world has ever known. Their extraordinary talent for organization produced monument after monument; their spiritual insight coupled with their manual skill created some of the world's finest art. Their system of government ran smoothly (with only two breakdowns; see chart) for 2,500 years.

Quick to learn and to adapt to his environment, the Egyptian was essentially practical rather than imaginative. He created a calendar to meet his needs, which he passed on to other civilizations. We use it today. He learned to do wonderful things with a piece of string. By knotting it he could accurately create a true right angle, design a wall painting, measure out a pyramid, fashion a net for catching fish or birds. But he did not indulge in much theory or speculation, like the Greeks. He knew precisely where he was going after he died—to the after-life. During some periods this was considered to be an exact replica of the life he was living on earth; at other times the concept was different. His imagination expressed itself chiefly in his lyric poetry, his adventure stories, and his art.

A sense of order prevailed in government, a triumph of organization along simple lines. After King Menes united Upper and Lower Egypt, he divided the land into thirty-eight sections, called *nomes* by the Greeks, each in the charge of a deputy, or *nomarch*.[1] The king kept in touch by traveling up and down the river, or sending emissaries to collect taxes. (These consisted of grain and produce, not money. There was no monetary exchange until late in the New Kingdom.)

From earliest times the pharaoh was considered owner of the land of Egypt. Easy communication helped maintain this unlimited power.

In the third century B.C. a scribe named Manetho wrote the first chronicle of Egypt. His work, *Aegyptiaca*, divided the succession of kings into dynasties, or royal families. This convenient pattern has been used by historians ever since.

As the country prospered, cities grew up along the bank of the Nile: Memphis, the first capital, whose patron was the god Ptah; Abydos, a holy city because Osiris, god of growing things, was said to be buried there; Heliopolis, city of the sun. But

[1] Some historians believe that the nomes represent the remnants of small prehistoric kingdoms. Others feel that the division of Egypt into nomes developed gradually after the unification.

the most magnificent of all cities was Thebes, which became capital of Egypt in the Middle Kingdom. In the days of growing affluence, Thebes, "city of a hundred gates," became known all over the civilized world. In 1200 B.C. the Phoenician king upbraided a sailor for bringing him so little gold, considering "the wealth of the city of Thebes." Later, Homer was to write about "Thebes of Egypt, where treasures of greatest store are laid up in men's houses." (*Iliad*, LX)

At the waterfront the docks teemed with ships, coming from the north with cargo and barges and from the south with building blocks. Across the river was the Valley of the Kings, the barren valley where pharaohs were buried. Between Thebes and Karnak stretched a long avenue leading to the temple, with its frowning pylons—the largest temple structure ever built.

No wonder there was sometimes boredom in the provinces. "I sit still, while my heart hastens away to see how things are faring in Memphis," a distracted lady writes. Birds and flowers were all very pleasant, but we can permit her a yawn or two.

When Herodotus visited Egypt in 470 B.C. he saw things that made him gape. Thebes was certainly not like Athens; Egyptians were not at all like Greeks. Herodotus traveled from the Delta to the First Cataract, taking copious notes. His observations are exact when he is able to observe for himself; he left us a clear explanation, for example, of how a mummy is pre-

Nubian captives and their overseers are depicted in this tomb painting. Museum of Bologna.

pared for burial. He is less accurate when he depends on the word of an over-enthusiastic guide.

"Men stay at home and do the weaving; women go abroad and are employed in trade." (Not necessarily true. Some men were excellent weavers; some women took up trades, but very few.) "Men carry burdens on their heads; women on their shoulders." (Both did both. Perhaps a lady wanted to save her hairdo.) "Other men live apart from beasts; but the Egyptians live with them." (Did he see a family cat scuttling across a garden wall?)

Herodotus continues in the true spirit of Greek antithesis for several pages. Washing went on inside—privately; eating went on outside—publicly. (There were no public baths like the ones in Greece; toilets and tubs were discreetly hidden behind four walls. As for refreshment, outdoor taverns were probably welcome in a warm climate. A teacher once chided a pupil: "Thou goest from tavern to tavern, the smell of beer marketh thy path. Men avoid thee when thou staggereth in the streets.")

Herodotus' report, which comes in Book II of his *Persian Wars,* was impressive. We must remember that he was writing from the point of view of a country just approaching the peak of her civilization. Egypt's greatness was well on the wane, some of it was only dimly remembered after a thousand years. Old customs prevailed, to be sure, but Herodotus must have listened to accounts of fierce hippopotami, strange ceremonies, and half-legendary heroes with amused interest. "I give you the story," he seems to say, "but I don't believe it."

The sights he marveled at are those we still marvel at today; the line of pyramids built over the centuries with such painstaking skill; architecture on a grand scale; temple walls covered with strangely beautiful hieroglyphic symbols; any number of small, useful things, fashioned with impeccable taste—all these reflected a genius for workmanship, but more important, the ability to enjoy the results of that work. In terms of true civilization, the ancient Egyptian had a talent for living.

chapter **4**

HATSHEPSUT, PHARAOH-QUEEN

"Hatshepsut has been called the first great woman in history. She simply appointed herself king of Egypt and that's all there was to it."

Will Cuppy, *Decline and Fall of Practically Everybody.*

T HE Nile waterfront at Thebes was a scene of wild commotion. Queen Hatshepsut's five ships were coming into port, returning from a trading voyage of several months to the land of Punt on the Red Sea.

Sailors, obviously enjoying the stir they had created on the wharfs, waved at the throng of noisy, cheering people. Some of the lively cargo from the expedition was very much in evidence. Monkeys chattered in the riggings; a panther howled; big white dogs barked. A few dark-skinned families stared over the railings as people pointed and shoved to get a better view.

Legend has it that the idea for the expedition came to the Queen while she was praying at the altar of Amon, the god of Thebes. "The ways of the land of Punt shall be explored," the god had said to her, "I will lead the expedition by water

This decorative scene adorned Hatshepsut's tomb near Thebes. Museum of Cairo.

. . . and by land, that it may bring forth wonderful things."

An expedition to Punt—what an idea for a prosperous, expanding nation! It had all the attractions of our modern sorties into outer space, and it was exactly like Hatshepsut to mastermind the whole thing. What she desired most deeply were myrrh trees she had read about in records of ancient voyagers. She needed them to adorn her temple, in the process of being built on the west side of the River Nile. From these trees came the precious essence of myrrh (the same as that brought by the Wise Men to the Christ child in Bethlehem) which was used in temple ceremonies.

Hatshepsut was getting her trees—and much more. Neshi, her treasurer and the commander of the voyage, had the goods brought for the Queen's inspection: lapis lazuli, ivory, leopard skins. He was proudest of all to present thirty-one live myrrh trees in pots. They had survived the long journey and would be transplanted to the temple gardens.

Hatshepsut's first act was to give thanks to Amon for the success of the voyage. The god's prophecy, "You shall create a land of Punt in Egypt," had been fulfilled.

Now comes the mystery. Where *was* this fabled land of Punt and how did the Egyptians get there? Some historians say that the Queen's five vessels probably sailed north from Thebes to

(Left.) Queen Hatshepsut is seated in this red granite statue. The Metropolitan Museum of Art.

(Below). Egyptian women used handsome mirrors such as this one in bronze. British Museum.

an old Middle Kingdom canal at the base of the Delta, where they crossed to the Gulf of Suez and headed south along the barren, sometimes treacherous Red Sea coast. More recent research reveals that there was then no navigable canal from the Delta to the Red Sea. The expedition would therefore have had to sail to a point on the river where they could unload and trek across the desert to a seaport. There, vessels more sea-worthy than the Nile boats could be obtained to take them south.

How far south they went no one knows exactly. Some scholars claim that Punt was in Somaliland, on the east coast of Africa. Others place it on the southwestern tip of Arabia. There were no accurate records, no maps. But the fact that they concluded such successful trading negotiations with the king of Punt, trekking back across the desert with all those animals and those thirty-one pots of myrrh trees, is remarkable in itself. Viewed in the light of its age, the Punt expedition was a tremendous undertaking—inspired by a god, organized by a woman, and later recorded in pictures on the walls of Hatshepsut's temple. That is why we know about it today.

The prime instigator of the expedition was a woman of forceful personality. She wanted all to believe that she had been claimed by Amon for his own, right from the beginning. We have a relief of her mother, Ahmose, sitting demurely beside the god, who announces: "Hatshepsut shall be the name of this my daughter whom I have placed in thy body. She shall exercise excellent kingship in this whole land." This was probably carved for Hatshepsut's temple after the fact—to strengthen her claim to the throne.[1]

At fifteen she married her half-brother Thutmose II, and they ruled for a short period. Upon his death, his son by a com-

---

[1] Hatshepsut did not have a clearly defined claim to the throne. As her nephew had been crowned king, a queen in Hatshepsut's position would normally have played the role of regent. She would not proclaim herself king, nor prevent her ward from exercising the kingship after he was of age. Egyptian queens did not really co-rule with their kings; it was the king who ruled.

moner was designated to become Thutmose III.

That's when the trouble started. Since the boy was too young to ascend the throne, Hatshepsut acted as regent. Years went by; the king was never allowed to rule. For twenty years Hatshepsut managed to keep Thutmose out of the picture; he remained so until she died. It can be assumed that the young man was not very fond of his aunt. In fact, he detested her. It must have been quite galling to see her being crowned pharaoh with all the pomp and circumstance of a man, and wearing on her head the high double crown of Egypt.

What could anyone do in the face of this whirlwind personality? Servants cowered, nobles bowed, vassal kings sent tributes. Hatshepsut was one of those women, not unlike Queen Elizabeth I of England, who fought to gain her position and having gained it, lived for her country. Her reign, like Elizabeth's, marked a time of prosperity, a period of cultural expansion. Strong-willed, ruthless, shrewd, energetic, she knew when to capitalize on her feminine qualities and when to suppress them. To the force of a man she added the wiles of a woman.

After Hatshepsut was crowned pharaoh she ordered many statues made of herself—some as a male, without breasts, wearing the symbolic pharaoh's beard. Other statues are feminine, showing a determined wedge-shaped face with delicate, regular features. In the huge statue of the Queen as a sphinx the face is quite recognizable on the enormous crouching lion's body.

She was a woman of plans and projects, all on a vast scale. When the voyage to Punt turned out successfully she turned her mind to other trading possibilities. Natural resources interested her and she sponsored development of the flourishing copper mines on the Sinai Peninsula. No warrior, she shrewdly stayed away from military affairs and put her mind on the peaceful enrichment of the country. Egypt enjoyed a tranquility it hadn't known in years.

Everybody worked. "Egypt was made to labor with bowed head for her," old Ineni, her father's architect, commented when this female dynamo ascended the throne. Building projects were everywhere. Temples which had been falling to pieces were restored. Public buildings were repaired and set to rights. But the real marvel was Hatshepsut's own temple, built into the massive tiger-colored cliffs on the east side of the Nile. This graceful structure of white limestone is striking against its background. The double row of colonnades is not like the usual massive Egyptian architecture; it anticipates the lightness and rhythm of Greek temples.

In the dramatic temple of Deir-el-Bahri Queen Hatshepsut was buried.

On the walls we can read the story of the Punt expedition and also follow the account of moving the huge obelisks Hatshepsut had set up in front of the temple of the god Amon-Re at Karnak.[1] She had a special fondness for these tall, thin, slightly tapering pillars with pyramid points at the top. They made splendid monuments on which to carve accounts of her great achievements.

Egypt had had women rulers before, princesses in the direct

[1] Obelisks, often decorated with records of the king's achievements, were primarily offerings to the sun-god Re.

royal line, who bestowed their royalty on their husbands. The husband then became pharaoh. As queens their function was to perpetuate the dynasty. The position of women in Egypt in those days has been compared to that of middle-class women in nineteenth-century Europe. The Egyptian woman could go about as much as she pleased and she could even get an education of sorts if she persisted. There are a few records of women scribes. In other respects, she had equal rights with men. She could inherit property, she was given full burial rites, and she could look forward to the same fulfillment in the afterlife.

In art a woman was glamorized—perpetually young, perpetually desirable. As the goddess Nut, she symbolized the sky; as Hathor, marriage and love; as Isis, the mother-goddess of civilization; as Sekhmet, the lion-headed goddess of strength and power.

The Pharaoh-Queen accepted all these roles. An inscription on a monument reads: "Her majesty grew beyond anything; to look upon her was more beautiful than anything; her form was like a god, she did everything, like a god, her splendor was like a god, her majesty was a maiden, beautiful, blooming."

We do not know which admirer composed this tribute. Do we detect a few fine flourishes from the pen of Her Majesty herself?

After she suppressed her young nephew, Hatshepsut backed up her position by another shrewd move—she surrounded herself with competent male advisers. In addition to the trusted Ineni, whom she had inherited from her father, she employed Neshi, her treasurer, to carry out the voyage to Punt, as already noted. She depended heavily on Hapu-Seneb, her vizier-priest, to direct the business of the temple. But the man on whom she bestowed her special favors was Senmut, architect of her temple.

Senmut is one of history's enigmas. He had eighty different titles. He lived in closer contact with the royal family than any commoner had ever done. As tutor to Hatshepsut's oldest daughter, he was constantly in and out of the royal household. There are several statues of him holding the child in his lap, protecting her beneath his cloak.

The temple Senmut had designed for the Queen at Deir el Bahri was an architectural gem; if he did it himself, he was a genius, well ahead of his time. He apparently thought so too and took what steps he could to escape anonymity. Over and over again, he carved his name, never prominently, but in obscure corners: "I, Senmut, created this for the glory of Queen Hatshepsut." He also thought far enough ahead to have his own tomb built near the Queen's.

The career of Senmut, although remarkable, is still shrouded in mystery. We know that he overcame his handicap of lowly birth and rose to become the most powerful official in Egypt. Then something happened. All we can be sure of is that the tomb he had built for himself near the Queen's was badly mutilated and the representations of himself which he had carved on the temple were erased. This was a grievous thing to do to any man, because it was thought that his enjoyment of an afterlife was entirely dependent on their preservation. Could it be that he had these carvings made in the Queen's temple without her consent? Or did he fall from her favor during her lifetime? We can only speculate.

After the Queen died, her name, too, was methodically hacked away from her monuments and it's not hard to guess who did it—Thutmose. By the time his men finished their destruction there was not a statue, not a hieroglyph, left to remind him of his hated aunt. (Fortunately archaeologists have been able to piece many of them back together again.)

Work on Hatshepsut's tomb was called to a halt and never completed. This was the final act of desecration.

Some say—and here we are confronted by another historical mystery—that Thutmose murdered his aunt, or had her done away with. She was in her fifties when she died; this king in name only had been kept waiting in the wings for twenty years.

Did his patience finally give out? Or did this power-hungry female, with the ego and drive of a modern tycoon, simply die of overwork?

We will never know. Look at the statue of Thutmose III seated on his throne. It will tell you nothing. Thutmose had his hour and he was to make one of the ablest pharaohs Egypt ever had. But there are no signs of a power struggle in his bland, assured face.

In the Metropolitan Museum there are three statues of Hatshepsut—one, a huge crouching sphinx, the other two, demure, enigmatic ladies seated nearby. Perhaps something whispers from the cold stone: There were two sides to this extraordinary nature, both powerful. Here was someone to be obeyed. Here was someone to be remembered. Here was someone in whose veins flowed the blood of the great pharaohs.

Eternal Friends

In the vast Metropolitan hall
A Sphinx reclined upon haunches
Paws extended, solid, benign.
When skipping across the court's tiles,
Came a dark girl of three, face alight
As if she knew she had recognized someone
She knew in a life now forgotten.
She crouched antlike before the huge form,
Stroked its paws, regarded its size
Without a vestige of fear.
Did a secret pass between
The ancient, inanimate figure
Of Hatshepsut, the Theban Queen,
And the vivid, wondering child?
Perhaps long ago in some temple
At the height of old Egypt's splendor
Before this commanding symbol,
She had once made the same obeisance.

Laura Benét (*New York Herald Tribune,* 1959)

With a member of his court, Pharaoh Thutmose III, appears on the
painted wall of this chapel dedicated to him. Museum of Cairo.

The ruins of Saqqara, near Memphis, have long attracted archaeologists,
for here the great Zoser pyramid was built.

chapter 5

THE WORLD'S MOST
SPECTACULAR TOMBS

"Too low they build, who build beneath the stars."

Edward Young, *Night Thoughts.*

Hatshepsut and her successor, Thutmose III, were among the early rulers who opened the door which eventually led to Egypt's greatest period of prosperity. We call it the New Kingdom. About 1,200 years before her time, probably around 2700 B.C., there lived an extraordinary man named Imhotep. He was a person of great learning who had risen to be the vizier, or right-hand man, of King Zoser, one of the kings of Egypt's first great period, called the Old Kingdom or Pyramid Age.

We know little about Imhotep, except by reputation. The King apparently thought highly of him because he put him in charge of the work on his tomb. He also sought his advice on matters of state. Later generations looked upon him as a great philosopher, scientist and healer. For centuries Egyptians

Model of a rocker or sled used to move building stones. British Museum.

King Zoser in this statue has a stiff, almost rigid, posture and is wearing a wig. Museum of Cairo.

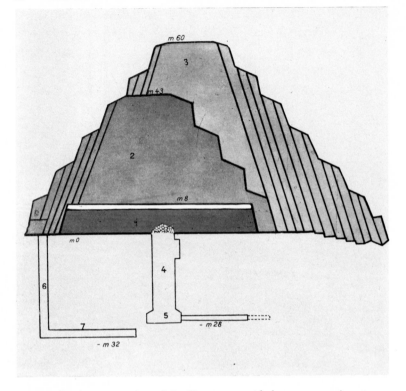

Longitudinal cross-section of the Zoser pyramid shows successive stages
of construction.

were to revere Imhotep as the "wise old man" of former days.
And in far-off Greece, a nation still to be born, Imhotep, the
healer, was later to be worshipped as a deity.

Such a man casts a long shadow. As a rule, we can only
speculate about the human being whose personality is obscured
in the mists of time. But in Imhotep's case we have an over-
whelming reminder of his greatness. Commissioned to create
a more stately mansion for the Pharaoh's soul, Imhotep designed the first pyramid. He was the first great architect whose
name is known to us.

The pyramid shape must have seemed new and striking. Yet
we can see how Imhotep evolved the idea. Before his time

kings and nobles had been buried under flat, rectangular brick slabs called mastabas. The body was laid away in a private chamber under the ground, often with a complex of antechambers around it to house funerary equipment. A rich noble might require sixty rooms in his final resting place. Once in a while he would proclaim his importance by having a smaller mastaba placed on top of the original, like a square-layered wedding cake.

King Zoser apparently wished to top his predecessors for all time. Imhotep designed for him a structure of six enormous mastabas, one piled on top of the other, and tapering off at the top. The whole mass rose in a series of stages, or steps, to a height of two hundred feet, and is today known as the Step Pyramid.[1] It was a bold design and it certainly must have attracted attention, rising like a stone mountain out of the flat desert at Saqqara. But this wasn't all. Around his giant masterpiece Imhotep erected a group of beautiful buildings of limestone, including two mastabas for the royal family. Ruins of columns show the same fine fluted effects to be seen in Greek columns some 2,500 years later. The wall of another building has straight, clean lines, in the mode of modern architecture.

King Zoser was pleased—or should have been. What better way to proclaim one's worth than to build a mountain in one's own honor? Less than a hundred years later Egyptian architects had learned how to build smooth-sided pyramids, based on the step design with the corners filled in. At both Saqqara and Giza on the west bank of the Nile the flat landscape began to be etched with triangular silhouettes. Marvels of accuracy, the pyramids were to be listed by the admiring Greeks as one of the seven wonders of the world.

The largest of the Giza pyramids belongs to the Fourth Dynasty king Khufu. It covers almost thirteen acres at the

[1] The origin and exact meaning of the pyramid-shaped tomb is obscure. Earlier mastabas had, on occasion, a stepped structure buried with them. Such monuments were perhaps the inspiration for Zoser's Step Pyramid. It is possible that the pyramid was thought of as a staircase by means of which the king might ascend to heaven.

base, measuring a half a mile around.   The architects had now learned how to construct a perfect pyramidal form by using much larger blocks of stone than previously.   Two million blocks went into the building of the Great Pyramid of Khufu. The first-quality white limestone surface covering the poorer-quality blocks was honed to a smooth polish.   The sharply pointed apex was then covered with a gold alloy, which picked up the rays of the sun and made the pyramid stand out sharply against the blue sky.[1]

Today most of the facing has been stripped for re-use, showing the step construction beneath.   An intrepid sightseer who climbs to the top of the Great Pyramid can examine the stones and see that they have been fitted together with such precision that a knife blade cannot be inserted between them.

How could all this have been achieved?   Herodotus wondered, too.   We can imagine him staring up at the giant structures, questioning the *dragoman,* much as the modern tourist does.   Fortunately he kept meticulous notes.

It took 100,000 men twenty years to build the pyramid, Herodotus was told.   Apparently the men worked in shifts; every three months the team was changed and a new one was pressed into service.

Contrary to what we have come to believe, these workers were not slaves.   The overseers may have been strict, but they were not cruel.   The men were fed well, housed decently, and sent back to their farms when it was time to plant crops or harvest them.   There is evidence that they took pride in building their mountain, much as the stonemasons in the Middle Ages took pride in building their cathedrals.   A few sections bear scribbled autographs on the stones—"The Lively Gang," "The Robust Gang"—as though the team couldn't bear to have its prowess go unnoticed.

One of the marvels of the pyramids is the transportation of

[1] It is thought that the capstones of some pyramids were overlaid with gold, but we are by no means sure of it.

The majestic columns in this hall at Saqqara rose over 30 feet in height and show papyrus-like fluting.

materials.   The big blocks of limestone came from quarries on the opposite side of the Nile.   Expert masons cut them from living rock, using stone hammers, copper saws, and jeweled drills.   When the Nile was at flood they floated the blocks across the river on enormous barges, coming as close as possible to the site.   Then they dragged them on sledges to the pyramid.

Next came the task of lifting the huge stones into place. Since it took forty men to lift one stone, this could be a problem, especially as the pyramid rose higher and higher.   But by this time builders had learned the usefulness of the ramp for easing a heavy stone uphill.   They found that any object would slide more readily over a wet surface.   They mastered the use of the rope, of levers, and of rollers.

Engineering knowledge was limited to these basic principles. Egyptian builders had no dray horses, no block and tackle, no calipers, no T squares.   Although they had no leveling instruments such as carpenters use today, they made excellent use of a simple device called a plumb bob, a small, heavy weight fastened to a cord and suspended to indicate a vertical line. They achieved their surprisingly accurate measurements with knotted string and sighting rods.

But as we look at these incredible marvels of precision and strength, we realize that the greatest art possessed by the Egyptians was that of organization.   To plan and execute on such a grand scale must have taken not only the genius of a few minds, but also the combined efforts of untold numbers of people working in harmony toward a single goal.   This is what staggers the imagination.   Four thousand years later, when the records had been lost, the wealth stolen, and the language forgotten, people were to ask, "How did they do it?"

Today there are about eighty pyramids in Egypt, none as large as the Great Pyramid, some quite small by comparison.   A few have fallen into decay; some were never completed.   The most spectacular ones are clustered at Saqqara and Giza, and they date from the Third to the Sixth Dynasty of the Old Kingdom.

A modern artist's conception, based on archaeological studies, demonstrates a temple under construction.

(Above.) Enclosure walls at Saqqara with Great Pyramid in background. (Right.) Amenhotep II. Egyptian Museum of Turin. (Below.) The Great Sphinx.

As a consequence, we call this period the Pyramid Age.

If you climb the 137 steps to the top of Khufu's Great Pyramid you get a striking view. Men and camels appear like ants, or people seen from the top of a forty-story building. Far in the distance, Cairo is a gray blur and the Mokattam Hills rise pale blue out of the desert. You look down on the head of the Great Sphinx, now shrunk to pygmy size, and two other pyramids. Following the line of palm trees, you see the green oasis of the Nile, crawling slowly northward. And to the west, always the desert, an infinity of dull, flat gold, extending, as the Bedouins say, "for a march of a thousand days."

Inside the pyramid is quite a different story. You go in through a tiny slit of an entrance, out of the baking sunshine into the sudden chill of a tunnel. This leads downhill. Then you turn abruptly and begin walking uphill toward the great hall and the King's chamber. You are deep inside the pyramid, with several million tons of stone over your head. In spite of electric light bulbs for tourists, you can sense the dark, the remoteness, the eternal silence. This is no place for the living.

The burial chamber, seventeen by thirty-four feet, seems pathetically small compared to its massive carapace. And it is doubtful that King Khufu's mummy ever resided here. Toward the end of his life he seems to have mistrusted his conspicuous tomb; his sarcophagus was never finished.

By 1500 B.C., most pharaohs realized that a pyramid or a temple, while it may have been good publicity, also attracted unwelcome visitors. What stronger temptation to a gang of thieves than a huge edifice containing a king's ransom, or a royal mummy whose garments were embedded with jewels? To confound the robbers the pharaohs decided to separate their actual places of burial from their funerary temples.

Across the river from Thebes, in a barren, rockbound valley, there came into being a new burial ground, later called by the Arabs the Valley of the Kings. Here, in inconspicuous little openings in the rock, royal mummies were sequestered, far from their mortuary temples.   Thutmose I was the first of forty pharaohs to be buried in the desolate little valley.

Those who presided over the interment were sworn to secrecy.   We have a note from a famous architect, Ineni, who planned the tomb of Thutmose I: "I inspected the excavation of the cliff-tomb of His Majesty—alone, no one seeing, no one hearing."

Yet there were those who saw, those who heard, those who betrayed.   Workmen must have been sorely tempted.   Priests, appointed guardians of the temple treasures, were often corrupt. By the beginning of the Eighteenth Dynasty, according to one writer, there was hardly a pyramid or a tomb that hadn't been looted of its wealth.

This fact is amazing when we consider the lengths to which clever architects went to protect their treasure.   Trapdoors, blind corridors, false doors, even false sarcophagi failed to deter the intruders.   The thieves were clever too, and as the ages wore on, the whole thing seemed to become a game of hide-and-seek.   A royal tomb was a challenge.   Robbers worked together in gangs; they went into business with the loot they found, became rich, passed trade secrets down from father to son.   A skilled professional, Amenupfer, who lived around 1000 B.C., has left this candid statement of how his outfit worked:

"We went to rob in accordance with our regular habit.   We opened their sarcophagi . . . and found the noble mummy of this king . . . completely bedecked with gold . . . We set fire to their coffins.   We took their furniture, articles of gold, silver, and bronze and divided them among ourselves."

But there remained things the robbers could not steal: the imagination, the logic, the admirable discipline which produced the Egypt of the Old Kingdom.   These great monuments bear witness to a type of mind which had learned to dedicate itself to a project of long duration.   In their stupendous feats of engineering these early builders had developed patience and reverence—both infinitely more precious than gold.

chapter 6

FIRST ARCHAEOLOGISTS IN EGYPT

"History has many cunning passages,
    contrived corridors
And issues, deceives with whispering
    ambitions,
Guides us by vanities. . . ."

                                    T. S. Eliot, *Gerontion.*

IN the middle of the nine-
teenth century everybody seemed to be searching for something.
In America, hopeful forty-niners were struggling toward
California—and gold. In England, Charles Darwin was poring
over his impressive collection of fauna and flora in preparation
for his revolutionary book, *The Origin of Species.* In France,
a group of painters, later to be called Impressionists, were
experimenting with the effects of light on color. In southwest
Africa, explorers were pushing their way toward a lake which
would be called Victoria—one of the sources of the Nile.

In Egypt, in 1850, a young Frenchman named Auguste
Mariette stumbled over a sphinx. This happened almost literally. Napoleon's invasion of Egypt early in the century had
created a widespread interest in antiquity. Scholars were learn-

Statue of a young man was found in the tomb of Ty, excavated by Auguste Mariette. Museum of Cairo.

ing to read ancient Egyptian writing and Mariette, an assistant curator at the Louvre, had been commissioned to buy as many papyrus scrolls as he could get his hands on.

When he got to Egypt he found himself far more interested in ancient ruins and genuinely distressed about their state of neglect. Signs of depredation and decay were everywhere. Hordes of curiosity seekers were beginning to visit Egypt. Souvenirs, real or fake, could be bought, or stolen, and dealers were only too willing to cooperate.

One day, while poking about on the site of an ancient cemetery near Cairo (now known as Saqqara), Mariette came upon the head of a statue sticking out of the sand. Although the features were eroded, he noticed a resemblance to some sphinxes he had seen in private gardens and on temple grounds, crouching creatures with human faces and horns growing out of their heads. If this *was* a sphinx, what was it doing all by itself? And where was the rest of it?

Brushing away the sand, Mariette inspected the head more closely and made out an inscription having to do with the sacred bulls of Apis. Something clicked in his mind. The horns—the hieroglyph. . . . He recalled the famous Avenue of the Sphinxes, mentioned in ancient records, but never found.

The only way to find out was to dig. And digging cost money. At this point Mariette could very well have given up, writing off his discovery as just another crumbling ruin which people passed by twenty times a day. His job, after all, was to buy papyrus.

Fortunately for archaeology he didn't give up. He apparently had no qualms about spending his government's francs on a gang of Arab workmen whom he hired to clear away the drifted sand. Gradually a figure came into view, its crouching position following the classic lines of a sphinx. Taking careful measurements, Mariette directed his workers to a spot a few feet away. They found another. They repeated the process and found still another. After two months' digging they had cleared the famous avenue, 140 sphinxes in all, each with bull's horns, enigmatic face, and crouching body.

The sight was so dramatic crowds gathered to see it. The discovery was so important it excited archaeologists all over the world. What could Mariette's superiors do but forgive him for spending his papyrus allowance on picks and shovels? People were gradually waking up to the fact that Egypt held more secrets than had ever been preserved in written records.

Artifacts continued to come to light bearing symbols of Apis, the sacred bull, revered in one of the many animal cults which flourished after the end of the New Kingdom. Where did the avenue lead? There must be more to look for.

Mariette's men continued to dig. After eight months of what he calls a "continual fight" against sand, heat, and cave-ins, someone's pick struck against something hard—a stone slab. It proved to be a door which led to a vast complex of corridors.

Then came one of those chilling moments of discovery an archaeologist never forgets. Mariette wrote in his diary: "When on the 12th of November, 1851, I went inside for the first time I was overcome by a feeling of astonishment, which even after five years I still remember vividly."

Peering into the darkness he could see giant sarcophagi, not for pharaohs, but for bulls which had been mummified with the rites of kings. The coffins, over twelve feet long, six feet wide, and nine feet high, were in separate chambers and had been plundered.

All but one. Mariette writes: "By some inexplicable accident, one room in the tomb of Apis . . . had escaped the robbers and I was lucky to find it, in fact, 3,700 years hadn't changed it. Fingerprints of the Egyptian who had placed the last stone in the wall across the door were still clearly marked in the cement. Someone had left footprints in a layer of sand in the corner of the mortuary chamber . . ."

Mariette might well have shivered, standing in the dark, half-understood world of strange cults and primitive forms of worship. The giant sarcophagi ranged along a passageway over 350 feet long. The area, called by the Greeks the Serapion, or place of the sacred bulls, is an impressive sight.[1]

Then and there Mariette dedicated his life to further search. Not far from the Serapion he found the tomb of Ty, a nobleman of the Old Kingdom. On the walls of Ty's tomb artists had recorded scenes from his everyday life in such detail that a viewer could almost feel that he was looking through a family photograph album, with a diary at his elbow.

The example of Mariette's tireless efforts convinced the Egyptians that they themselves should make some effort to save what was left of their country's precious ruins. Statues and temples were becoming half buried in sand. Tombs were being stripped of their precious contents. The old scandal of grave robbing was bad enough, but its modern version, traffic in antiquities, was even worse because it involved the collusion of tourists and collectors. It was time the government stepped in.

The Egyptian Museum was founded, and Mariette was made chief of all excavations. This move provided a central clearing-house for all activities. After his appointment, all discoveries, all projects, were to be reported to the museum.

Auguste Mariette never lost his zeal for things Egyptian, which appears to have been romantic as well as scientific. An interesting sidelight on his career is that he provided the plot for the opera *Aïda*. As Conservator of Antiquities he had been asked to suggest a suitable subject to commemorate the opening of the Suez Canal in 1869. He came up with a romance about a Nubian princess in love with an Egyptian general who was already betrothed to the pharaoh's daughter. The triangle ends in tragedy, of course. Giuseppe Verdi, the composer, liked Mariette's idea and immortalized the lovers in impassioned arias, duets, and a world-famous march.

---

[1] The Apis bulls were buried because the god Ptah was thought to dwell in them. In other words, the god became material in the form of a bull, and in only one bull at a time. When the bull in which he lived died, the god was reborn in another bull.

The entrance to the tomb of Ty follows a long passage.

(Below Left.) Everyday life inspired artists. Here a man is washing. Museum of Cairo. (Below Right.) A harpist, in terra-cotta, was painted. Museum of Cairo.

When Mariette died, he was buried in Egypt, and his body lies in a marble sarcophagus.

About thirty years after Mariette discovered the Serapion, a sharp-eyed mathematician aged twenty-seven arrived in Egypt with the announced intention of measuring Khufu's Great Pyramid. His name was William Matthew Flinders Petrie; one day he would become professor of the new science of Egyptology at the University of London.

Petrie, too, was skilled with the pick and shovel. Like Mariette, he suspected that the secrets of the past lay under the sands of the desert. He had been a solitary, solemn little boy, preoccupied with his rock collection, and a student of the exact sciences. He grew up and published a book on the science of measurement. His father, fascinated by some of the fanciful notions then current about the construction of the pyramids, urged his son to find out more about them. Had these enormous rock piles been built "from above" as one wild theorizer claimed? Did Egyptian builders have magic powers? Was there an answer to the riddle of the pyramids?

There was an answer, and it was NO. No riddle. No magic powers. The Great Pyramid had been planned, measured out, and built like any vast architectural work, from the ground up, with painstaking care, stone by stone, by teams of disciplined workers. These facts the practical, no-nonsense Petrie was to prove beyond a shadow of a doubt.

With his cookstove, lamp, and cot, he created a base of operations in an empty mastaba near the Great Pyramid and began his colossal task of measuring.

Much of the time he worked alone. Anyone passing the Great Pyramid at dusk might have been astonished to see the naked figure of a man disappearing into its shadows with his light and his box of tools. Petrie's best chance of working undisturbed was to start when the sightseers had left and the sun had gone down, and keep going until dawn. Clothes hampered him, so he simply took them off. He spent hour after hour in the hot, fetid atmosphere—measuring, analyzing, taking notes, then checking measurements, checking notes, making more notes. The Great Pyramid was being subjected to a more searching analysis than it had undergone in 4,000 years, since the day when its architects had planned and built it.

Life underground was something of an ordeal for Petrie. Breathing dust, working by lamplight, crawling about on his hands and knees, he learned to look for clues to the past in even the smallest stone. In doing so, he set down the cardinal rule which archaeologists and detectives have followed ever since: never move or destroy a piece of evidence until it has been recorded.

His flair for practical mathematics, very like that of Egyptian builders, stood him in good stead. Although the Great Pyramid had nothing mystical about it, it was no less remarkable as an incredible feat of engineering accuracy. "The squareness and level of the base," Petrie wrote, "is brilliantly true, the average error being less than a ten-thousandth of the side in equality, squareness and level."

Having established these matters to his own satisfaction, Petrie knew that his career lay in Egypt. He must find out about other pyramids. One of the most tantalizing to his imagination was a huddled brick mass near the Nile, surely the ruined pyramid of a king. But whose? No one knew.

The pyramid was in such poor shape that no entrance was visible, sand having piled up around the base. Petrie began digging around the most likely spot, at the north. No luck. He tried another side. Still no luck. Frustrated, he decided to bore a large hole at an angle down through the masonry until he came to an open space. Since no pyramid was solid, there had to be a room inside.

This unorthodox decision was a lucky one. As he surmised, his tunnel led to a wider space. Could it be the burial chamber? The passage was too small to admit the head and shoulders of a man, so Petrie decided to send "a thin and active lad" in ahead of him.

This lad, whoever he was, deserves special citation from historians. Equipped with a flashlight and rope tied securely around his middle, he was lowered foot by foot into the inky blackness. What a relief it must have been to touch firm ground! As the boy flashed his torch around he could see that he was in someone's burial chamber. There were two sarcophagi, both empty.

Petrie was delighted with this report. Even though the tomb had been plundered, it was worth investigating further. He enlarged the passage and went in himself. He found a few artifacts, among them a broken piece of alabaster vase, on which was inscribed a royal cartouche—Amenemhet III, a Middle Kingdom pharaoh. The identity of the tomb owner was clear.

At this point Petrie might have been well satisfied to pack up his equipment, pay off his workmen (not to mention the thin

Sphinx of Amenemhet III, Middle Kingdom. Museum of Cairo. This damaged head of Amenemhet III is an exceptionally fine sculpture of the period. Museum of Cairo.

lad), and go home. But it was not in his make-up to leave problems half solved. Where was the true entrance to the pyramid? He resolved to keep on digging until he found the plan of the original builders.

If he had had any idea of what he was in for he might have changed his mind. Surely his workmen had second thoughts as they pushed their way through blocked-up passages, followed blind alleys, forced open trapdoors that led nowhere. Unlike the Great Pyramid, Amenemhet's tomb seemed like something a giant rat had created, gnawing and tearing its way in bewildering twists and turns through the masonry.

To make matters worse, some of the galleries were partially flooded. River seepage had created barriers of sheer mud. Here is Petrie's account from his diary:

> Up to the east passage the muddy earth rose nearly to the roof, and we had to crawl through. At the south end of this there seemed to be no exit, but a slight gap under the S.E. trapdoor showed that there was a way; and clearing out some earth I got in far enough to stick tight, and knocked the candle out. Matches had to be fetched, as we were streaming with the heat, so that nothing could be kept dry in the only garment I had on. Under the stone I got into the S.E. chamber and then the south passage was so nearly filled with mud that we had to lie flat and slide along it propelled by fingers and toes.
>
> At last I reached the S.W. chamber. The blind passage being level did not promise a way out; the lean lad got up on top of the first trapdoor . . . and waded through the water to the antechamber. There at last I found a passage sloping considerably upward and knew that we were in the entrance passage.

Petrie found his front door at last, in the least likely place, the south side. It had taken him months of grueling work. Despite his weariness, he had to admire the shrewdness of the architects, who must have thought they had hidden the body of their pharaoh.   As he dug and dredged and crawled and turned back, he realized that grave robbers had been ahead of him.   They had been just as shrewd, just as persistent as he.

Thus this brilliant, methodical, tireless man discovered things in Egypt he didn't know he was looking for.   In finding out how a pyramid was built, he learned not a little bit about the fine art of tomb robbery.   He figured that it must have taken a well-organized gang of accomplished men months, or even years, to do such a thorough job on Amenemhet's buried wealth.

Whoever the robbers were, they must have been as tough, relentless, and alert as bank robbers.   Some gangs were known to have included local families; some must have had the co-operation of corrupt priests, hired to guard the premises.   Every generation produced its own underworld characters and the motive was always the same—wealth.   These belong to a dark side of Egypt's history.

Petrie continued to dig and sift and analyze.   As his friends put it, he literally "scratched his way through Egypt."   As he grew older he came to look something like an Old Testament patriarch, with his high forehead, penetrating eyes, and flowing white beard.   Visitors, who occasionally found their way to his "digs," were scandalized at his informal way of roughing it on the desert, dipping into cans of food when he was hungry, ignoring physical comforts both for himself and for his staff.

But tea party refinements were not for this dedicated searcher who eventually became the grand old man of archaeology. Petrie lived into his nineties.   His great contribution to this new science was his strict application of scientific method.

This method was not new; it had been applied in the early part of the century when men first struggled to read the curious symbols on Egyptian monuments.   But no one had been successful until a young scholar named Champollion cracked the secret of the hieroglyphs.   It had taken both imagination and logic to solve the mystery.

chapter 7

A HIEROGLYPHIC RIDDLE

"A boy's ear is on his back. . . . He listens when he is beaten."

From a papyrus on the teaching of scribes.

IN the summer of 1799 one of Napoleon's soldiers, digging a few miles east of Alexandria near the village of Rosetta at the mouth of the Nile, came upon an odd-looking slab of black stone. It was about three feet high and had been used as a part of a support for a wall. The surface was smooth, obviously not the same material as the adjoining masonry. It was covered with indecipherable hieroglyphs, what seemed to be some ancient writing.

The soldier grew curious. He was undoubtedly aware of Napoleon Bonaparte's passion for antiquity; every man in the ranks had heard about the general's thundering comment as they marched past pyramids and giant statues in the desert: "Soldiers, forty centuries look down on you!"

He showed the stone to his senior officer, who ordered it

shipped to Alexandria.   Neither man realized that this slab, later to become famous as the Rosetta Stone, would prove to be one of the greatest archaeological discoveries of all time, a key to unlock countless mysteries of the past.

What made the inscription so invaluable was that it appeared to be written in three parts, all possibly saying the same thing and one of which was well-known and could be deciphered.

The known part was in Coptic, a form of Egyptian written in Greek letters.   From their knowledge of Coptic, scholars were able to translate the inscription, which was devoted to praising the works of Ptolemy V and was written in 196 B.C.

The second version was in ancient hieroglyphs, a language of which scholars already had some knowledge.   The third inscription, however, was couched in characters which seemed

This limestone statue of a scribe has been painted.   Louvre.

Fragment of papyrus describes a medical problem during the 18th Dynasty. Leipzig University.

both peculiarly strange and incomprehensible as well.

But by working from the Coptic with the help of further clues from the ancient hieroglyphs, it then became possible to start work on deciphering the meaning of the third. The last named proved to be a popular form of hieroglyphic writing called Demotic.[1] Since Demotic, at a later period in Egyptian history, was to gain wide usage in Egyptian daily life, understanding of it was to prove useful in gaining further knowledge.

The discovery created a stir locally. The French army paper, *Le Courier d'Egypte,* gave it full coverage and then raised an important question: Could the three languages on the Rosetta Stone provide the key for the decoding of the ancient picture writing of the Egyptians?

Now Napoleon himself became interested. He ordered the inscription copied and distributed to linguistic experts and

[1] Demotic is a kind of shorthand version of a species of hieroglyphics called hieratic. It is a cursive form—one in which the letters are joined together.

The Rosetta Stone enabled Jean-Francois Champollion to decipher the mysterious hieroglyphic writings. British Museum.

antiquarians alike in hopes that someone among them would be able to solve the puzzle.

That same year, in the town of Figeac in southern France, a nine-year-old boy named Jean-Francois Champollion was beginning to attract attention as an unusual scholar. He had a knack for languages and a burning curiosity concerning ancient life. When the news of the Rosetta Stone was released to the world, Jean-Francois boasted to his brother, an archaeologist, that some day he would find out how to read hieroglyphics.

The lad seemed to be uncannily suited for this destiny. He not only had the brilliance and sense of purpose, but oddly enough, he looked slightly Egyptian. Many people were impressed by his dark skin, dark hair, and slightly slanted eyes, which eventually earned him his nickname of "the Egyptian."

By the time he was in his teens, Champollion was well versed in Coptic. This was to be of great help to him in solving the riddle of the hieroglyphics.

Champollion knew this and the language became an all-consuming passion. He read all the Coptic texts he could find; he took notes in Coptic; he even prepared a Coptic dictionary. "My Coptic dictionary swells daily," he wrote his brother, "not so its author." This poor boy lived in great poverty in Paris when he was getting his education and probably went hungry more than once.

Then came the first breakthrough. Thomas Young, a London scientist, deciphered the name *PTOLEMY* in the ancient text. It appeared several times, always surrounded by an oval called a cartouche, which Young believed—as others had before him—signified a royal name. With the help of another bilingual text, Young then decoded a cartouche of *CLEOPATRA*. He could now see similarities in certain symbols.

This was something to go on—but Young got no further. Nothing else seemed to make sense. He had been working on the generally held theory that each hieroglyph was a literal picture of an object. When Champollion came up with the completely new suggestion that some of the symbols might represent sounds, Young was skeptical. Who was this upstart who thought he could thread his way through a maze that had baffled older men for years? He'd had no training in the scientific method. Furthermore, he had absolutely no proof.

Then, one day, Champollion produced a small, but indisputable piece of evidence—a hieroglyph of *RAMSES* composed of symbols which were part sound, part picture. Young had to admit that the idea had merit.

Champollion, according to the popular story, received his insight in a flash, after months and months of intense effort. An impetuous young man, he burst into his brother's study shouting, *"Je tiens l'affaire!"* ("I have it!"), which reminds us of Archimedes' triumphant cry of "Eureka!"[1]

[1] Thomas Young had identified the hieroglyphic signs for "f" and "t" and determined that different characters could have the same sounds. It was Champollion who conclusively proved that the hieroglyphic system was basically phonetic and not a purely symbolic system of writing.

This scene took place in 1822, twenty-three years after the discovery of the Rosetta Stone.   But it was clear that scholars were now on the right track.   They eventually discovered that a hieroglyph could represent not only a picture, a sound, or syllable, but also an idea, or concept.   The sun symbol, a disk ⊙, could mean *sun, day, light,* or *time.* A picture of an eye could mean *pleasant.*   A picture of a hippopotamus could mean *heavy.* A man on his knees could express, among other things, the idea of prayer.

Unfortunately Champollion did not live to see the end of his work.   He died when he was only forty-two.   Language

A hieroglyphic inscription showing the god of the sun and his boat, from the Tomb of Seti.

scholars learned a great deal from his work and eventually came to understand another important factor in ancient hieroglyphics—that meanings of words changed whenever the symbols were followed by certain other symbols, or "determinatives."   A determinative simply put a word into its proper context.   The hieroglyph for *beautiful* (one of the commonest in the Egyptian language) changed its meaning to *young woman* when followed by the determinative, a kneeling female figure. Accompanied by other determinatives, it could take on as many as eight different meanings.

Another problem that harassed archaeologists was the lack of guides in conventional word order. In hieroglyphic writing words were not separated from each other, nor were there any punctuation marks. Hieroglyphs could be written from right to left or left to right—horizontally in lines and vertically in columns. Writing from right to left, however, was most common. Signs having fronts and backs, such as animal figures, face toward the beginning of the line of text in which they occur. These proved to be valuable clues to the sequence of the writing.

When hieroglyphics began to make sense, enthusiastic scholars went up and down the Nile, "reading" Egypt from Rosetta to Abu Simbel. They pored over papyrus scrolls, some in poor condition, but many preserved and still readable, thanks to the dry climate. They scrutinized the carvings on temple walls and in tombs. It was slow, exasperating work, but it brought results.

By degrees, the history of this ancient, enigmatic country began to unroll before the eyes of an amazed world. New light was cast on the mystery of the pyramids. Historians found out who had built them, and why. From two sets of King Lists, one found at Abydos and another, much later, at Saqqara, it was possible to construct a chronological record of pharaohs in their proper dynasties.[1] Historians have also found out about actual events, modes of life and conquests, although there is still much to be learned. The Battle of Megiddo (called Armageddon in the Old Testament), an important Egyptian victory in Syria, was described in detail on the walls of the temple of Amon at Karnak. Its hero, King Thutmose III, naturally did not wish to have his exploits go unnoticed. The genius of Young, of Champollion, and of hundreds of dedicated scholars saved him from oblivion.

[1] The King Lists were far from complete. In themselves they did not offer enough evidence for a reconstruction of the dynasties of Egypt. Recently scholars have used all kinds of data, both archaeological and textual, to set up a sequence of kings and events.

Letters, tax records, poetry—even formulae for magic—helped to shed light on the past. Among the most illuminating discoveries were the scrolls left in tombs, known as the *Book of the Dead.* These scrolls provided scholars with information on funerary rites and the Egyptians' concept of the afterlife.[1]

A particularly valuable set of archives turned up in Amarna, Akhenaton's brief, ill-fated capital. They were clay tablets, not hieroglyphic, but stamped in the wedge-shaped cuneiform script of Mesopotamia. They contained messages to the Pharaoh from provinces in Syria. Many of them besought him to come to their aid and drive away intruders who were harrying their borders.

But the preoccupied young monarch, bedazzled by his beautiful new city and his radiant god Aton, probably never answered the messages.[2] The Amarna letters are as pathetic as they are revealing, and they tell us a great deal about the state of the empire in the Eighteenth Dynasty.

If it seems miraculous that we ever learned to read the Egyptian language, it must have been a difficult task for the Egyptians themselves.

The seated figure, shown earlier, writing materials at hand, with an expression of undoubted intelligence in his face, is a scribe, a familiar subject in Egyptian sculpture, a beloved figure in Egyptian society. This man, who had spent years learning his profession, held a unique place. He could not only write and read, he could also calculate and transmit messages. This

[1] The term *Book of the Dead* can be misleading. It refers to papyri placed in tombs. These papyri are actually collections of "magic" scrolls which people believed would enable the deceased to journey in safety to the Netherworld and to receive in the afterlife what he wanted.

[2] Akhenaton, although not very active militarily, was hardly a complete pacifist. There is some indication that at the end of his reign he was planning a military expedition into Asia; and it is possible that he actually led a campaign. In any event he had no moral objection to being shown as a military man; for even if he never led an army, he permitted himself to be represented slaying the enemies of Egypt. The gradual discovery of blocks from Akhenaton's temples, decorated with scenes of varied subject matter, continually reminds us of how little we know about this period of Egyptian history.

set him above artisans, who worked only with their hands.

Learning to draw the complex set of hieroglyphic symbols wasn't easy. If a boy wanted to master it, he began young. Methods of instruction were simple, if uninspired. Children simply copied each character and were kept at it until they could do it perfectly. This was difficult, because the slightest error in a line could change a meaning. No one knows exactly how many characters there were; the numbers varied with the passage of years, but they certainly went into the hundreds. The Egyptians, for example, had twenty or more hieroglyphs for birds. Imagine learning to draw each bird without error!

Materials were simple. Papyrus was expensive and hard to manufacture, so children were given small pieces of limestone shard called ostraka, which they probably used like slates. Pens were fashioned from reeds, with the points slashed to make a soft nib which made a graceful, flowing line when dipped into mineral powder, or lampblack, dissolved in water.

As soon as a boy mastered the individual signs, he was given entire texts to copy. In this way he went through a whole curriculum of geography, history, physiology, arithmetic. In mathematics he had only to learn addition and subtraction. The Egyptians never figured out how to multiply or divide. Their numerical system was accurate so far as it went.

Picture a room full of boys, ranging from about four to sixteen years of age, sitting in rows on hard benches, or squatting on the floor, copying, memorizing, chanting texts, day after day after day. In front of them, a row of earthenware pots with neat rolls of papyrus sticking out of them; brushes of all sizes; pots of ink; clay tablets, too, for in the New Kingdom, when communication with Syria was frequent, a scribe had to learn cuneiform symbols as well as his own script. The tedium must have been unbearable for a boy who liked to hunt and fish or play ball. But a stern master, equipped with a switch,

Carrying the materials used by scribes slung over his shoulder, a man faces a table on which food has been placed. Museum of Cairo.

kept order. Discipline was swift and forthright. Instruction
went on relentlessly for about twelve years. After that, a young
man, if he had applied himself, could be called a scribe.

There are on record many injunctions to children to submit
to this ordeal. They must have had many temptations to join
the army, to live the life of a sailor, or to get a mechanical
job, just as boys have today. Some of the persuaders shame-
lessly resort to snob appeal: "Be a scribe . . . that you may go
forth admired, in white attire, and that courtiers may salute
you."

Other injunctions simply back into the subject, assuring the
boy that if he works now, he can relax later: ". . . you do not
have to carry a basket; you do not have to ply an oar . . . you
are not at the beck and call of many masters. . . ."

Very often a parent taught his own sons the basic elements
of his craft, or sent them out to be apprenticed. In the case
of scribes, a select nucleus often formed around a tutor. A
pharaoh usually employed a teacher for his children and bright
sons and sometimes daughters of nobles frequently joined the
group. Schools grew and by the New Kingdom there were
several schools for scribes in Egypt.

Once he became a scribe, a young man's future was up to
him. He could be anything from a humble village letter writer
or accountant, to a specialist in legal documents, or a priest,
or a doctor. He could hold an important position in the
pharaoh's household—supervise the treasury, become overseer
of works. Architecture offered him rich opportunities because
the planning and supervising of monuments, especially for a
monument-happy king like Amenhotep III or Ramses III,
never stopped. As supervisor of builders, a scribe towered over
the illiterate masses.

A man named Akhthos wrote to his son: "Learn to be a scribe
for this will be of greater advantage to you than all the other
trades . . . One day at school is helpful to you and work done
there will endure for an eternity, like mountains."

chapter  **8**

"YOUNG FOREVER . . ."

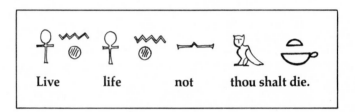

Live   life   not   thou shalt die.

. . . Book of the Dead.

"**Y**OU will live again. You will live again forever. Behold, you are young forever!"

The priest has ceased his chanting, coming to the end of a long ritual for a man who has died. The mummy, prepared and wrapped for burial and propped upright, awaits the final act of the ceremony. The widow kneels at its feet, while behind her other priests and a file of mourning women play their roles in the solemn funeral rites before the tomb.

Now comes an act of curious significance—the opening of the mouth, or reanimating the vital force, so that the dead person can speak, move about, eat and breathe in the afterworld just as he did on earth. One priest stands directly in front of the mummy, tilting a jar of purifying liquid over the mouth. Another wafts incense. In silence, a third priest waves an

This ceremony, known as "Opening the Mouth," was illustrated in *The Book of the Dead.* British Museum.

odd-looking stick angled at one end like a carpenter's adz. This is the instrument which will symbolically open the man's mouth to renewed life. The people weep. Again the reassuring words: "You will live forever."

The ancient Egyptians, like people in most civilizations, believed in life after death. But their view of the afterlife was, for the most part, strictly literal. They assumed that a person's body lived on in his tomb, even though the man himself traveled to a blessed place. They must therefore preserve the body, revere it, and keep it from harm.

Every Egyptian man and woman was believed to have a shadowy twin called a Ka, who may have protected him during his life and stayed close by in the tomb after death as guardian. Everyone also possessed a spirit, called a Ba which was often represented as a flower bud in the form of a human head. It could also be a winged creature with a human head, which was often painted on tomb ceilings. During the day the soul could fly where it liked, visiting places its owner had loved on earth. After dark it came back to the tomb, hovering over the body to ward off evil spirits.[1]

If a winged Ba couldn't find its proper tomb it could get lost. If a body disintegrated, a Ka would cease to exist. Therefore the Egyptians went to great lengths to preserve their dead by a process known as mummification.

Creating a mummy required the combined skills of many people and the whole procedure took two or three months. Embalmers often traveled from place to place, setting up their shops in tents near temples or the houses of the deceased.

[1] Egyptian religious belief is most complicated and little understood. It is thus difficult to discuss it in a short amount of space. An essential feature is the number of seeming contradictions. The Egyptians believed, for example, that the afterlife was similar to life on earth. But this did not prevent them from believing that it also was quite different. The deceased might live on in his tomb, but at the same time he might go off to the Netherworld. He might be content to live eternally as he had on earth; or after death he might become Osiris, lord of the Netherworld. Such contradictions are hard to explain. Perhaps they are not contradictions after all. Rather, each belief might represent a different approach to a common problem. We have, as yet, no certain answer to this question.

Bodies of men, women, children, sometimes animals, were all embalmed in the same way, although the quality of work varied with the price.

The first step was to make an incision in the side of the corpse and remove the internal organs (all except the heart). The gray matter of the brain was carefully siphoned out through the nostrils. The liver, lungs, stomach, and intestines were set aside in separate vessels called Canopic jars, to be embalmed separately and placed in the tomb.

To preserve the body itself the embalmers impregnated it with a substance called natron (something like salt), which quickened the process of drying out. In the arid atmosphere of Egypt drying did not take long. They then bathed the corpse, annointed it with pine resin, and packed the body cavity with wads of linen soaked in resin.

The next stage was the wrapping, which took both patience and skill. Strips of linen had to be wound smoothly around fingers, toes, arms, legs, and finally the whole body, exactly like a bandage. In the mummies of the rich, precious stones and amulets were frequently embedded in the layers, with more resin added to make them stick. A well-wrapped mummy required as many as twenty layers of bandage, the strip being from two to eight inches wide. Like good householders, people saved their old bed linen for this purpose; marks of the former owner often appear in corners, faded from repeated washings.[1]

The bandaged mummy was now ready for burial. Meanwhile, hundreds of artisans had been at work constructing a series of coffins, or sarcophagi, to contain the body. They fitted inside one another like a nest of boxes, the innermost ones usually shaped like a person, with the face painted on the top.

If the mummy was royal he wore a gold mask, with his beard, his crown, and the royal cobra of Egypt in the center of his forehead. A pharaoh had three or four coffins, and perhaps

[1] This description from Herodotus applies to mummification at its peak of perfection. It does not hold true for all periods. The art was a long time in developing.

(Below Right and Above.) Sandals made of palm and a chest filled with toilet articles were left in a tomb for the afterlife. (Below Left.) Pomegranates and fruit of the palm. All in the Egyptian Museum of Turin.

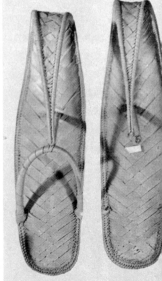

a stone sepulcher. King Tutankhamon, whose funeral was the last word in opulence, had seven coffins.

Coffins were usually of wood, overlaid with gold and painted in brilliant colors, often embellished with semiprecious stones. Artists frequently painted an eye, or a pair of eyes, at the end where the head was so that the person in the coffin could look out. On some coffins we see representations of doors which would allow passage to the afterlife.

The path was long, and a dead man needed instructions on how to find his way in the afterlife. A set of Pyramid Texts, therefore, carved on the walls of pyramids in the Fifth and Sixth Dynasties, warned of monsters lurking in the deep, on the way to the afterlife. They explained how the passenger might assume another shape for his own protection, if necessary. Thus he would safely pass through the "twelve gates of night (death) and the twelve gates of day (life) and ultimately reach the blessed land."[1]

No wonder a man's funerary rites took seventy to a hundred days! It was no easy trip to eternity. When all was ready a procession of priests, relatives, friends, and mourners followed the coffin, borne on a sledge, to the tomb. Many carried gifts of food, tomb furniture, the dead man's possessions prized in life. He often had a "sky boat," perhaps in which to make the journey across the heavens—quite logical when we consider that the Egyptians spent so much of their time in boats.[2]

After the Eighteenth Dynasty, a period when Egypt was

[1] As the Egyptians believed that the written and spoken words were magically charged with power, they probably served not only as a guide for the deceased or as a set of spells for him to read, but they also guaranteed that what was contained in the spells would come to pass. What was written, magically *was*.

[2] The exact meaning of these boats is unclear. Because they often came in pairs, it was thought that they were solar boats, as the sun-god Re had one boat for traversing the heavens by day and another for crossing the Netherworld by night. This makes good sense for the deceased king, who is thought of as sailing with Re. But Khufu had *more* than two boats, and this is baffling because we haven't enough evidence to say that anyone but the king could sail with Re. Several boats in a tomb could either be pleasure boats for the afterlife or models of the boats used in the deceased's funeral. The question cannot be answered.

wealthy, small models of servants were buried with the mummy, so that they could go on working for the master in the next life. These figures, only a few inches long, often shaped like mummies, were called *shawabti*. They came into being in the Middle Kingdom. No one knows the origin of this curious name. A hieroglyphic inscription on one of them announces: "I am reckoned to do any work ... to cultivate fields, to irrigate the banks, to transport sand of the west to the east ..." The shawabtis were there to do any work which might be expected of the deceased.

No more heavy loads; no more fetching and carrying in the afterworld! Here is every man's dream of a long vacation.

But the work on earth was by no means over. The mummy might be safely sealed in his several coffins and provided with his celestial road maps—but the family's job was not finished. The bereaved held frequent services in the outer chamber of the tomb. They had to see that the place was kept clean, and that offerings of fresh flowers and garden produce were supplied for the Ka. They had to keep the place guarded so that thieves couldn't break in and desecrate the sacred objects. Tomb upkeep was arduous, time-consuming, and costly.

As the number of tombs increased, it became increasingly difficult to look after them properly. The older tombs, especially the tombs of rich pharaohs, became an easy prey to

Scales are shown in this line drawing from a Giza tomb of the fifth dynasty. Science Museum of London.

robbers. This was sad because the continued existence of the spirit depended on the existence of the man's image, or name, whether mummy, statue, relief painting, or written inscription. If these were all destroyed then the spirit had nothing to return to and was itself destroyed.

It was up to the gods to judge the worth of the person who had died. He must appear before a tribunal of forty-two assessors and convince them that he had led a blameless life. His assertions of innocence bear a resemblance to Old Testament Commandments:

> I have not done injury to mankind.
> I have not cursed the God.
> I have not caused illness.
> I have not lessened the corn measure.
> I have not carried off milk from the
> mouth of a babe.
> I have not driven away cattle, which
> were in their pastures.

The *Book of the Dead*, a collection of papyrus scrolls from tombs in the Eighteenth Dynasty, gives the complete list of moral affirmations, together with information on the journey to the afterworld and other wisdom literature useful to the dead. Several gods were involved in the final meeting. The chief was Osiris, god of the underworld (represented in mummy form), who acted as judge. Tomb paintings show a man or woman waiting for judgment as Anubis, the jackal-headed god who presided over embalming, weighs the heart on a scale against a feather, symbol of truth. Thoth, god of wisdom and scribes, had the head of a wading bird like a heron, called an ibis. He records the verdict on a tablet.

If the deceased person passed this test he was admitted to the blessed afterlife. If not—we can only conjecture. There is no Egyptian hell. In all of Egyptian religious writing we hear little about torment after death, or purgatory, or persecu-

Hieroglyphics embelish this page from the *Book of the Dead* with Anubis in the foreground. Museum of Cairo.

tion of the damned. Those who didn't make it were vaguely "doomed to roam the earth," but their wanderings were unspecific, had no special form.[1]

In one judgment picture, just underneath the scales of Anubis, a fearsome creature crouches on its haunches, looking up at the heart with bared fangs. The accompanying statement is abundantly clear: "The devourer waits."

About the afterworld itself there was little speculation; it was simply a mirror of the present, with the more niggling earthly cares smoothed away. Egyptians seemed to have a talent for enjoying the moment. They were not restless seekers after goals that did not exist. When life ceased, a person wanted to catch happiness he had known and hold it. He wanted to go on enjoying his garden; he wanted to sail on the river, to cherish his family, to do exactly as he had been doing.

To be sure, there were stories, old legends, hints bearing strong suggestion of the fascination of the unknown. The puzzling fragment called "The Shipwrecked Sailor" beckons to a vastness just over the rim of man's mind. It goes like this:

A ship headed for the king's mines across the sea was torn to pieces in a frightful gale. Everyone on it was drowned with the exception of one young man, who grabbed a large piece of wreckage and managed to stay afloat.

[1] To a great extent, Egyptian religion either denied the existence of death or sought to defeat it. Nevertheless the Egyptian, and certainly the king, could and did (at least in some periods) hope for more in the afterlife than he had had upon earth.

Eventually he drifted to an island, an enchanting place with waving trees, green grass, sparkling lakes and rivers. The sailor could hardly believe his luck. His first act was to build a fire and make a sacrifice to the gods in thanks for his rescue.

Suddenly a huge serpent appeared. Its shining scales almost blinded the sailor as they caught the rays of the sun. Out of its almost human face glittered dark, piercing eyes. It wore a beard like a pharaoh's. "Who are you who dares to come to my island?" the serpent demanded.

The sailor was too terrified to speak. To his amazement, the serpent lifted him gently and carried him to his cave. Here the sailor managed to stutter out the story of his mishap. If the serpent would only set him free, he promised that his pharaoh would send him rich rewards.

The serpent only smiled. "You are on the Island of the Blessed," it said. "I am its ruler. I do not need the gifts of your pharaoh."

The sailor was puzzled. Who would dare refuse a pharaoh's gifts? But the serpent would not reveal any more. It gave the sailor presents, assuring him that a ship would come and that he would be home in two months.

It happened exactly as the serpent promised. When the ship arrived, the overjoyed sailor begged the captain to let him report his marvelous experience to the pharaoh. In a flash of insight he realized that this had been no earthbound adventure. The island he had visited had been no ordinary island; it was the island of the Ka, the blessed place where no man goes, except after death. . . .

Here the story breaks off. We are left to ponder its profound symbolism—the boat, the beautiful land, the miraculous rescue, the bearded prophetic serpent. It has the teasing elusive quality of a dream.[1]

---

[1] Egyptian religion had its share of what seems to us the fantastic. In "The Shipwrecked Sailor," however, "Island of the Ka," need not refer to the place where the deceased go after death; it might simply mean an island where there is food to live on. It is hard to tell if this story was as mysterious to the Egyptians as it is to us.

The ruins of the temple of Amon at Karnak.

chapter  9

BUILDERS, SCULPTORS
AND PAINTERS

"Behold the heart of His Majesty was satisfied with the making of a very great monument."

From an inscription on an ancient stele.

THE desert sun beat down on the waiting crowd gathered on the flat plain. The people laughed and talked among themselves, occasionally pointing to a roped-off area, empty save for some wooden stakes, a few workmen's tools, and piles of building stones. Suddenly the word went round: "The Pharaoh is coming!"

The crowd grew silent. People stood on tiptoe; children were swung to their fathers' shoulders to get a better view of the Pharaoh, who was about to make one of his rare public appearances. Preceded by his standard-bearers, he was carried aloft in his chair of state.

The people broke into a cheer. The stately procession threaded its way to a selected spot and stopped. Priests fussily gave last instructions to the crew of royal builders. They in

The Pharaoh Seti appears in this fresco from his tomb in the Valley of Kings.

turn checked final details—baskets, jars, knives, and a large coil of twine. The building ceremony of the stretching of the cord, like our laying of the cornerstone, was about to begin.

A priest held up his hand for silence. The chief architect of the temple picked up the coil of twine (probably of papyrus fiber dyed red to stand out against the sand of the desert) and began to unwind it. He paced from stake to stake, tying the cord carefully at each angle, marking out the floor plan of the building. Here, the great hall; here the sanctuary; here a courtyard.

A scribe was reading from an inscription on a stele, or large slab, to be placed in the temple courtyard commemorating the event. He praised His Majesty's efforts and concluded, "Never has happened the like from the beginning."

Everyone cheered. Surveyors following the red lines now drew markers in the sand with picks, indicating where trenches were to be dug. Then priests took over. Wearing their ceremonial leopard skins, they walked through the squared-off areas of rooms and corridors, placing symbolic objects in small pits dug in various corners. Buried models of building tools, amulets, even food and wine would complete the dedication of the temple to the god.

"He made it as his monument for his father, Amon, Lord of Thebes, an eternal everlasting fortress of fine white sandstone. . . ." The voice of the scribe rose and fell as he went on to describe the splendors of the temple-to-be, the greatness of Amon, the god to whom it was dedicated, and the transcendent genius of the Pharaoh, who had caused it to be built.[1]

The ceremony was over. The Pharaoh was borne away on his chair. The crowd huzzahed, waved, broke up, went home.

[1] All temples were founded by Pharaoh, and the services conducted there were theoretically carried out only by Pharaoh. Egyptian temple reliefs show only Pharaoh worshipping and making offerings to the gods because only a god (the king) was worthy of, or capable of, dealing with the other gods. (In practice, however, religious services were carried out by Pharaoh's deputies: the priests.) Pharaoh's main role as ruler was to keep the gods well and happy so that they would make Egypt prosperous. What the gods required were homes (temples), food, and clothing.

They would be back in small, curious groups to watch the walls of the tremendous pylon, or tower-gate, slowly rise, as gangs of highly trained workmen heaved the huge blocks into place.

From earliest times, when people from the desert began to congregate in villages along the banks of the Nile, they built homes for their gods as well as for themselves. The first chapels, like primitive houses, had reed walls supported by bundles of tough reeds tied together to form columns. These columns were later imitated in stone, and the long flutings we see on pillars in later architecture are reminiscent of those early efforts. As time went on, and stonemasons increased their skills, the house of the god assumed more and more importance. Its planning and execution demanded the cooperation of men with many specialized skills in stone. The workers, like those who built the medieval cathedrals, were proud to have a part in the project.

They could also be assured of steady work for years to come. Building a House of Eternity, as the temple was called, could go on for generations, like the building of a pyramid. The project gave economic stability to the country.

When Champollion, decoder of the Rosetta Stone, first viewed the rows of huge temple columns he commented, "They thought in terms of people 100 feet tall." He wasn't far from the truth. The frowning pylon seemed calculated to frighten away anyone but a god, a priest, or a pharaoh. "Keep out," it said.

The people would never be admitted to the sacred precincts of the House of Eternity, which were open only to priests who served the god. But they would often visit a complex of buildings outside the temple called the House of Life. Here scribes copied texts, held workshops, and conducted schools. Doctors treated patients and surgeons performed operations. As the House of Eternity honored the god with its solemn festivals, so the House of Life served the practical needs of the people.

The ruin of the famous temple complex of Karnak is one

(Left.) An obelisk from the Amon temple at Karnak. (Top Right.) One view of the temple of Amon. (Bottom Right.) Osiris, the god of the dead, was frequently placed in tombs. Louvre.

of the largest in the world. Walking through it, one can get a fairly clear idea of its two typical features: its massive pylons and the long rows of pillars in its Hypostyle, or many-columned hall. These shafts of stone, looking like the trunks of giant redwoods, are so huge that a hundred men could easily stand on the top of one pillar. Archaeologists have been able to trace the growth of Karnak from a simple chapel to a bewildering complex of courtyards, gates, and outbuildings. The temple grew in importance as the city of Thebes became widely known through the civilized world. Pharaohs were fond of adding another gate, or a chapel, or a court—just another reminder of their greatness.

Egyptian temples weren't all enormous, but they all had the quality of simple, almost austere, dignity. The custom for kings to have funerary temples built separate from the tomb began in the Eighteenth Dynasty of the New Kingdom. The kings directed that their earthly remains be bundled off in secret to a remote cliffside called the Valley of the Kings. One of the most beautiful of these chapels is that of Queen Hatshepsut at Deir el Bahri. Its architect, Senmut, dramatized its terraces and its graceful lines of white pillars against a craggy backdrop of tawny-colored rock. Including the landscape in its design, it anticipates Greek architecture in feeling.

As though soaring columns and huge gates weren't enough, pharaohs were fond of setting up sixty-foot pointed shafts, usually in pairs, in front of temples to certain gods, especially Re or Amon-Re. These obelisks (derived from the Greek word for needle) were mined and cut, all in one piece in the quarries, then floated up the Nile on barges, exactly like building stones. Before they were set up, sculptors chiseled in hieroglyphs the exploits of the pharaoh on each obelisk. The pyramidal top was covered with a gold alloy so that it would glitter in the rays of the sun.

Erecting these tall shafts and getting them to stand straight must have been a problem. As far as we know, the Egyptians solved it by using their own simple principles—the ramp, the rope, the plumb line—as well as their incredible ability to organize manpower.

There are only a few obelisks left in Egypt, because they became fashionable trophies. Most of them were taken down during the Roman occupation of Egypt and set up in Italy. Others floated off to adorn the metropolises of the world—Rome, Paris, London, New York. Uprooting them and transporting them without damage must have been a problem, too. When the 200-ton Cleopatra's Needle was hauled to New York's Central Park in 1880 it cracked the pavements of Fifth Avenue.

Like the temple and the obelisk, outdoor statuary was created with the afterlife in mind. Huge statues glorified the pharaoh-who-was-god, or the god who was more powerful than all men put together. The Egyptian sphinx, an odd crouching creature with the body of a lion and the face of a human, symbolized strength. The Greeks gave it the name of Sphinx, or Strangler, on account of its resemblance to the mythological creature who lived on the mountain pass leading to Greek Thebes and who posed impossible questions to travelers. When they couldn't answer, it did them in most horribly.

There was nothing sinister, or evil, about the sphinxes of Egypt. They were simply embodiments of the sun-god appearing in pairs, or in impressive avenues leading to a temple.[1] During ceremonial processions they, too, must have served as fairly effective civic reminders of the pharaoh's power.

The Great Sphinx, bigger, older and more sphinx-like than the others, stands alone at Giza, a sphinx-unto-itself. Since it is unique in the world, it has come to typify Egypt. Its face, what is left of it, is said to be the likeness of the Fourth Dynasty King Khafre, whose crumbling pyramid rises nearby, and which the sphinx appears designed to protect. It has lived through

[1] While in the later periods the sphinx was identified as a solar deity, we are not sure if it had the same meaning in earlier periods. The sphinx may be thought of as a protective deity—reliefs show sphinxes trampling the enemies of Egypt.

many vicissitudes—sandstorms, predators, cannonballs from an emir who is said to have disliked its smug expression, bullets from Napoleon's soldiers, who have been accused of using it for target practice. The nose and part of the mouth are quite gone. Yet its expression of lofty detachment remains and if it has any thoughts, they might echo those of the philosopher who said "you dare not mock the Sphinx."

There was a statue that whistled. It was one of two hulking sixty-five-foot figures sitting side by side on the desert, mistakenly called the Colossi of Memnon by the Greeks, who confused them with one of their heroes who may have visited Egypt. They are actually statues of Amenhotep III, a New Kingdom pharaoh, and his wife. One of them used to emit weird moaning sounds after sundown and was deemed prophetic by the ancients. But alas, in Roman times a practical soul investigated and found a fault, or fissure, inside the stone. The air, forced out of the fissure with temperature changes, whistled as it escaped. The fissure was sealed and the sphinx was silenced.

These huge statues of Amenhotep III and his wife at Thebes were incorrectly called the Colossi of Memnon by the Greeks.

Not all statues were huge. Inside temples and mortuary chapels they were life-size and sometimes smaller. As Old Kingdom notions of the pharaoh-god shrank, so did the statues. But at the end of the New Kingdom there was a return of the bigger and better under Ramses the Great. Wanting to add as many cubits to his statue as possible, and as often as possible, he placed his image all over Egypt. His four seventy-foot statues at Abu Simbel fairly shout this message at the viewer. Around his shins cluster the small figures of his family, like dolls. Stinging sands and desert winds have eroded the four faces of Ramses, but not his Olympian calm.

To honor the dead man, sculptors carved bas reliefs, or the typically Egyptian "sunk reliefs" on the walls of his tomb or temple. These little stories in stone spoke of his pleasurable life on earth—his work, his play, his success in his profession, his family. In a sense, he was courting destiny by saying, "This is the way it was; this is the way I want it to be." Sculptors of bas reliefs followed the rule set down in early times—the

Enormous head of Ramses II, pharaoh of the New Kingdom, was found at Luxor.

principal figure large, his family and servants in miniature. The head and legs of a figure are in profile; chest and shoulders face the viewer full front, as does the eye, large in proportion to the features and accentuated by dark lines. This style had a purpose: to show the significant aspects of a human being, rather than to give a literal, realistic view of him, as the Greek sculptors did. A set of the well-developed shoulders, for example, strikes us forcibly, reminding us that these shoulders could heave huge stones, that they were the capable shoulders of a people who gave themselves completely to any task.

The wide-open eye communicates a different thought. Is it the yearning of every man to look beyond—where, we cannot say? Could the profile-on-straight-on effect be a primitive way of suggesting motion? These are busy figures, and it is simply entertaining to speculate as we seem to see a man in the act of turning. We watch him as he hunts, casts anchor, throws his stick, guides his oxen. As he works, he offers us his Picasso-like countenance. Now he's looking at us; now he isn't.[1]

As sculptors grew expert with the chisel they found that they could bring out subtle effects in bas reliefs by applying color. Experimenting first with colored minerals ground to a fine powder, they then found they could make the powder stick with wax, thus adding a lasting brightness to the carved scenes. Later they sketched their designs directly on the walls, guided by marked-off squares, like outsize graph paper. After the figures had been drawn, and carefully corrected, they were painted in shades of yellow, red-ochre, blue, green, black, or white. Backgrounds were washed in with white, blue-gray, and occasionally yellow, following the strict conventions in the use of color. A man's skin was always darker than a woman's.

---

[1] The Egyptians strove for completeness in their two-dimensional art. They wanted to represent objects as they knew them to be, with all their important features included in the view which showed them most fully. A man has two shoulders; hence a representation of a man should have two shoulders. An eye is more complete seen full-face while a profile displays more of a face than a front view. Egyptian figures are drawn, therefore, not from a single viewpoint, but with each part of the body seen from its most characteristic view.

The complexion of Osiris, or a mummy, often presents a green cast—to suggest not death, but rather the sprouting of corn and rebirth.

One of the most pleasing aspects of Egyptian art is its design. Even in the most primitive paintings balance and harmony prevail, as though the artist could hardly wait to report the beauty of the world as he saw it. The flat montage designs of vegetation and animals sometimes take us by surprise in their strong suggestion of nature. We can almost hear the sudden *whoosh* of wings as herons rise from the reeds, or the quiet lapping of the water as a boat is poled through a papyrus swamp.

There were a few attempts to create simple perspective, but an artist often summarized his background. Straight, parallel lines stood for a papyrus thicket, wavy lines at the bottom of a picture, for water. As artists learned to apply pigment in layers, they found that they could give the illusion of something "showing through" the paint. A lady's diaphanous pleated garment often reveals the lines of her body.

Strangely enough, many tomb decorations were left unfinished. No one has been able to explain why. It may be that, death being no respecter of persons, the occupant of the tomb required it and moved in before the artists had completed their elaborate designs. It may be that the Egyptians had a philosophy of incompletion—that they deliberately laid down their chisels and brushes after the man's spirit had left his body. The house of the Ka was now sacred, no fit place for working men. The portrait of the lady in the tomb of Usheret, at Thebes, suggests an abrupt stoppage of work. She has no ear, no eye. The half-completed design on her headband looks as if the artist had stopped in the middle of a brush stroke.

However this may be, we are fortunate to learn a great deal about techniques of painting by examining pictures in their various stages of completion. On the walls of the mastaba tomb of Peri-Nebi in the Metropolitan Museum of Art in New York, one can see behind the figures, if one looks closely, the faint reddish lines of the string which once marked guides for the designers.

Under King Akhenaton, in the Amarna period in Dynasty XVIII of the New Kingdom, figures were shown as more relaxed, more human, more individual, although many of the stylistic features had been introduced long before. The new school of art seemed to probe more deeply into a man or a woman, revealing human faults and failings. But this approach did not last. If we study the wall paintings, the furniture and the jewelry which turned up in the tombs of the New Kingdom, we can sense a change in Egyptian art. Simplicity has given way to opulence. It is an art which reflects life in a rich empire, rather than the somewhat restricted but simple and natural life in the Old Kingdom.

In some of the tombs colors remain, seemingly as bright as on the day they were painted; in others the paintings have begun to chip and peel, due to the effects of the atmosphere. How ironic to think that these stunning color effects were consigned to the tomb! The artists who executed these paintings (for the most part forgotten because they rarely signed their work) must have painted in semi-darkness with only torches to guide them. Neither they, nor the pharaohs for whom they worked, could have looked on the spectacular beauty of their creations in full light.

Yet the tomb painters lived in a sunlit land. All around them lay the splendors of Egypt. Surely they carried this notion of a land bathed in dazzling sunlight when they worked underground. What artists glimpsed with the inward eye, men with flashbulbs and cameras, some 4000 years later, were to reveal to an astonished world.

chapter **10**

SCIENCE AND MAGIC

Delicate gold pendant shows Osiris between his mother Isis and his son Horus. Louvre.

"Thus the analogy between the magical and the scientific conceptions of the world is close. In both of them the succession of events is assumed to be perfectly regular and certain, being determined by immutable laws. . . . Hence the strong attraction which magic and science alike have exerted on the human mind. . . ."

Sir James G. Fraser, *The Golden Bough.*

ALL was quiet in the House of Life. The surgeon bent over the still form of a man stretched out on a table. He listened to his heartbeat, felt his pulse.

"Bind the patient. Shave his head," he ordered his assistants. "We will cut into the skull."

A wail rose from the ring of tense watchers, relatives of the patient. A woman stepped forward. "My husband will die!"

The surgeon frowned. "Perhaps. And would you send him to the afterlife with an evil spirit lodged in his skull?"

The woman dropped her head and stepped back.

The patient was securely bound to the table and given a final draught of drugged wine. The doctor called for his instruments, which a young student had been sterilizing in a flame. He selected a knife and made a neat incision; another assistant

118

stepped quickly forward to stanch the flow of blood.   Then, using a small bronze saw, the surgeon slowly and painstakingly cut a section of cranial bone and carefully lifted it out.   With a pair of calipers he deftly probed inside.

"By Set and all devils, I think we have our evil spirit!   Come take a look!"

The students crowded around.   With infinite care the surgeon removed a large blood clot which had been pressing on the brain tissues.   Moving quickly and deftly, he fitted a silver plate into the space where the skull bone had been taken out.   He stitched the edges of the wound together and applied a linen bandage.

Once more he listened to the man's heart and pulse.   The patient stirred, groaned.   For a second his eyes flickered open in a bright, comprehending glance.

"Cover him well; give him wine when he can swallow.   With good care, he will live."

The man's wife burst into another wail, this time of joy. "Praise Amon!"   The patient was borne to a place of quiet as priestly helpers purified the room for the next patient.

The art of trepanning, or cutting into the skull, was practiced with amazing skill by Egyptian doctors, but not with unqualified success.   Brain surgery was frequently a last resort, performed when all else had failed to drive the evil spirit from the victim's body.   In the above incident the evil invader had appeared in the form of a blood clot, and therefore could be dispatched. If the patient was lucky enough to escape infection he would get well.

Although the Egyptians never matched the Babylonians in mathematics, they went far beyond them in the science of medicine.   The functioning of the human body had a special appeal for people who sought practical answers to human problems, not the least of which was illness.   The fame of Egyptian doctors spread all throughout the Mediterranean world.   They were often sent for, to heal royal patients in places as far off as the Syrian provinces.   Years later, the Greek father of med-

These magic symbols are carved in ivory. Louvre.

icine, Hippocrates, would draw on much of their wisdom for his medical texts.

Herodotus observed that "each physician applies himself to one disease only, and not more. Some physicians are for the eyes, others for the head, others for the teeth. . . ."

This early form of specialization is not so strange when we consider how much accurate medical knowledge the Egyptians already had. Centuries of preparing mummies for burial had taught them anatomy. They understood the circulation of the blood, although they had only vague notions of the functions of each organ. A young man who wanted to be a doctor spent many years as an apprentice in the House of Life, taking notes, learning methods, very much in the manner of a medical student today. In his profession he was bound to a strict scientific code; he could leave nothing to guesswork; nothing, that is, concerning which facts were obtainable. Experience, patience, and not a little skill went into the art of healing.

Trial and error came into the picture too. Treatments involved various drugs and concoctions, some of which were effective and some of which had little value. Physicians used castor oil as an emetic. They found out which herbs would alleviate pain, which herbs were stimulants.

In surgery they went to amazing lengths. They learned to classify and diagnose most common injuries; this we know from a remarkable document called the *Edwin Smith Surgical Papyrus,* named for the man who discovered it. Here is probably the first book on surgery ever written. It lists forty-eight cases of injury, including head bruises, fractures, sprains, and dislocations. It discusses splints, sutures, and methods of stanching the flow of blood. In summation, it requires the doctor to come to one of three conclusions when he makes his diagnosis: (1) An ailment which I will treat. (2) An ailment which I will try to treat. (3) An ailment not to be treated.

Let us suppose for a moment that the man with the blood clot had had an ailment not to be treated. What would have happened to him then? He would have been turned over to the priests who practiced special arts of magic in another section of the House of Life. They would have murmured chants, spells, secret formulas. They might even have served the patient a healing drink—a secret charm written down on papyrus and then dissolved in water.

It is hard to believe that such a practical-minded people could react with such incredible naïveté. But when knowledge gave out, magic took over. The Egyptian had no notion of what a germ was, or a disease; he simply saw its manifestations. Something dark and dreadful made him ill; if he couldn't deal with it himself he appealed to a higher power to prevail over the one afflicting him.

The religious side of his nature was more primitive, more trusting than his practical side. Magic was his link with the unknown. And being strongly visual and artistic, he simply drew what he wanted. In the Pyramid Texts of the Old Kingdom, every hieroglyph of a potentially dangerous creature was mutilated in some way to make it safe in the presence of the dead. The crouching lion is neatly severed in half; the scorpion pierced with arrows, assurance that he will never distribute his venom around the tomb again.

Like all primitive peoples, the Egyptians had a complex roster of gods and goddesses. Many of the first mythological deities had animal forms. Early visitors from the world outside were surprised to see the Egyptians worshipping what they thought were the animals themselves. But actually they were worshipping the gods whom they believed dwelt within the animals. The Egyptians evidently associated certain animals with specific functions or environments, and in turn assigned those functions to the gods within those animals. Jackals, for example, would be found at night in the cemeteries of the desert, which might explain the jackal-shape of the god of the cemeteries, Anubis. The goddess Hathor, the deity of nourishment and fruitfulness, was shown often in the form of a cow.

Perhaps the most interesting of all the Egyptian gods and the most prevalent was Horus, whose all-seeing falcon eye appears in countless places. Every pharaoh was considered to be an incarnation of Horus and bore a Horus-name in addition to his own. This god played a dramatic part in the old legend of creation. When he drove out his uncle Set, avenging the murder of his father Osiris, he became the savior of mankind. (Set, incidentally, remained on the lists as a convenient scapegoat. When the surgeon cried out, "By Set and all devils!" he was simply using a handy exclamation.)

Any number of animals came into the picture, usually in local cults. Bast, the cat, presided at Bubastis, her special city. A good half-dozen attributes were pinned to this evasive feline, the commonest of which was love. (The Egyptian word for the domestic cat was, appropriately, *miw.*) Sekhmet, a lion, or rather lioness, was looked to in times of war for her strength. But she, too, was unreliable, having an unfortunate tendency to cause epidemics and to team up with the other side if the whim seized her.

A town called Crocodilopolis proclaims the reigning deity of this particular locality. Sobek, its god, had a mouth large enough and teeth sharp enough to guarantee the respect of his worshippers. The mighty Apis, the bull, for whom the Serapion was built, was also a creature to be reckoned with.

Not all gods had animal forms. Osiris, hero of the creation legend, had a human face and often a mummified body, designating his lordship of the afterlife. Re, one of the oldest of the gods, wears a sun disk which represents the beginning of all things. In the New Kingdom his name was coupled with that of Amon, god of Thebes, and the worship of Amon-Re persisted through many dynasties.

The name Amon meant "hidden," befitting his high magical powers. He took on different forms—a goose, a ram, a king.[1] Connected with powerful pharaohs of the New Kingdom and a great city, Amon of Thebes was well-known throughout the ancient world.

Ptah reigned at Memphis, Egypt's old capital. According to some legends, Ptah was the one who created the universe, conferring the kingship on Menes, the first pharaoh. His royal consort was the lion goddess Sekhmet.

Images make direct appeal to the imagination. The pictorially minded Egyptians developed a written literature very early on account of their vivid symbols. From ancient papyrus rolls, fortunately preserved by the dry climate, we can see the two sides of the Egyptian mind: one accurate, methodical, practical; the other artistic, lyrical, expressing a love of life and a yearning to live it well.

The old stories of Sinuhe, the traveler, and Wenamon, the accident-prone sailor, were tales told around a campfire in the manner of all early tales, and later written down.[2] But it is through their lyric poetry that Egyptians show how deeply they cherished beauty—beauty of nature, beauty of love, beauty of

---

[1] Amon could be shown as human-shaped, although not necessarily as a king. Some scholars feel that the meaning "hidden" for his name indicated that he was once the god of the air or wind.

[2] The story of Sinuhe was indeed a popular story. "The Voyage of Wenamon," however, which describes a voyage to Byblos in Lebanon, may be, according to some, not a "story," but the description of an actual voyage.

mankind. The blind harpist sings to the guests at the banquet of what he can see only with his inward eye. Woebegone Romeo, who longs to see his Juliet, is frustrated with desire:

> Seven days to yesterday I have not seen the sister
> [loved one]
>
>   And a sickness has invaded me,
> My body has become heavy,
>   Forgetful of my own self. . . .
>
> When I see her I am well
> If she opens her eye my body is young again.
>   If she speaks, my body is strong again.
> When I embrace her she drives evil away from me,
>   But she has gone forth from me seven days!

A late philosophical work, called *The Instruction of Amenenopet*, contains some startling parallels to Old Testament thought. At the time when it was written, Egypt's greatness was beginning to fade. Wars and invasions had ravaged the land. People were beginning to find out what suffering meant, in a way they had never known before. The keynote of resignation as a prime virtue appears in their writings for the first time.

A lyric poem of an earlier period also takes on a note of melancholy, as the writer speaks the quiet thoughts of old age:

> Welcome is death to me today
> As a man yearns to see his home
> When he has spent long years in exile. . . .[1]

---

[1] The lyric poem entitled, "The Dispute with his Soul of One who is Tired of Life," is a long work which relates a man's attempt to convince his soul to stay with him through suicide. It describes the man's reluctance to live in a troubled time (probably the First Intermediate Period) and is a much older text than *The Instruction of Amenenopet.* By the time of the First Intermediate Period, the Egyptians had already learned what suffering was.

Compare this lovely metaphor of death from the Book of
Ecclesiastes:

> . . . and the grasshopper shall be a burden,
> and desire shall fail:
> because man goeth to his long home.

When a man died a set of papyrus "books" was usually placed
in his tomb. These papyri included much of the current wisdom as expressed in literature and poetry, as well as instructions
about getting to the afterlife. They were given the collective
title *Book of the Dead,* but they seem to have been in reality
a library for the use of the dead man.

Papyrus traveled well, and it was convenient for conveying
messages. The Syrian provinces were most certainly influenced
by Egyptian thought. These people had first learned to write

Both of these statues, the
one on the left of Sekhmet
and the one on the right of
Ptah, were discovered in
Tutankhamon's tomb. Mu-
seum of Cairo.

in the neat, efficient Babylonian cuneiform on clay tablets.   But eventually hieroglyphics found their way across the Isthmus of Suez with migrating peoples, and into their script.   The famous Phoenician alphabet, adapted by the Greeks, then by the Romans, undoubtedly had its origins in both.

As far as we know, the Egyptians were the first to write the outpourings of their emotions—love, joy, pain.   Their primitive way of doing it was to draw pictures with chisel, brush, and pen.   Their first writers were artists.

Thus it is that science and religion, reason and imagination, have always been two sides of a coin.   The doctor, in his zeal to cure his patient, the priest, in the performance of his rites, the blind poet, in his vision of a beautiful world—each in his own way reaches out to make mankind better.

But these two sides must remain in perfect balance.   The little seated goddess, Ma'at,[1] with the feather rising out of her headband, suggests this equilibrium.   Ma'at is often defined as "truth," but is perhaps more accurately translated as "divine order."   Because it was divine it applied to gods as well as men and was the governing rule of the entire universe.

To go against the order was to create its opposite, chaos or evil.   This was not only important throughout life.   At the day of judgment a man was examined to see how well he had abided by the divine order, and his afterlife was ordained accordingly.

In these words from a papyrus written on the accession of the Pharaoh Merneptah Ma'at evokes the ideal world:

Ma'at has overcome falsehood, the transgressors are over-thrown, the greedy are repulsed.   The water stands and fails not, and the Nile carries a high flood.   The days are long, the nights have hours and the months come aright.   The gods are content and light of heart, and life is spent in laughter and wonder.

[1] Also written as Mayet.

chapter

AKHENATON, THE SUN WORSHIPPER

"Ah, but a man's reach should exceed his grasp,
Or what's a heaven for?"

Robert Browning, *Andrea del Sarto.*

THE morning sun shone on the gleaming white walls of the new palace of the pharaoh, King Akhenaton. It warmed the sleek, dark heads of the crowd milling around in the courtyard. Its rays picked up the pale blues of lotus blossoms twined about the Balcony of Appearances, where the Pharaoh and his queen were about to show themselves to their people.

The balcony was empty, the curtains behind it drawn. But clearly something was about to happen. Akhenaton had declared his intention of greeting his people on this particular morning, along with his queen, Nefertiti, famed for her beauty throughout Egypt. Who would miss the chance of such an intimate glimpse of royalty, which in the old days had kept itself remote from ordinary people?

The pharaoh makes an offering to Aton, the sun-god. Museum of Cairo.

A man in the crowd nudged his neighbor and pointed to the symbol of a sun disk with rays reaching downward, symbol of the sun-god, Aton, embroidered in gold on the curtain. "Aton has blessed the building of this city, just as the Pharaoh promised. They say he will richly reward the city planners. My wife says that the Queen . . ."

"Shhh!" His neighbor shushed him. "Here they come!"

"Here they come!" The cry was picked up by one, then another, and another. "Hail Akhenaton! Hail Nefertiti!"

The curtains parted. Akhenaton and his queen stepped onto the balcony. The Pharaoh approached the railing and raised his arms toward the sun. "All hail Aton, bringer of light and life." He spoke solemnly, his voice curiously soft, as though he were feeling tremendous emotion. His thin, sensitive face, with full lips and pronounced chin, wore a half smile; it seemed the face of a mystic rather than a pharaoh. The expression it wore was that of a man who saw beyond the perception of ordinary men. Just behind him, Queen Nefertiti was smiling too, as she echoed her husband's praise of the god. Every man in the crowd, seeing the pure lines of her profile, must have vowed inwardly to serve his queen.

"Hail Aton, bringer of light and life!" Many voices picked up the refrain, using the familiar words of a hymn written by the King himself:

> Bright is the earth when thou risest in the horizon.
> When thou shinest as Aton by day
> Thou drivest away the darkness.

Then Akhenaton held up his hand for silence. He called his architects forward one by one and presented them with gifts for their work on the city. He rewarded artists for their fine paintings and bas reliefs. He paid tribute to all builders, gardeners, scribes, and priests of Aton, who had contributed their efforts to the success of the new city, Akhetaton, which had

taken almost two years to build.   Last of all he decreed that
Akhetaton, or Horizon of Aton, would henceforth be Egypt's
capital.   Those who had so willingly followed him here from
Thebes, Egypt's former capital, would continue to worship Aton
as their sole god.

Worship of one god was not a completely new idea.
Akhenaton undoubtedly became fascinated with the concept
when he was in his early teens after he heard about it from
priests in Heliopolis, a city where sun cults flourished.   They
made no statues of Aton because they believed that the essence
of the divine being was in the sun itself.   There was therefore
no personification of the god, not even any stories about
him—only the symbol of the sun disk, rays pointing downwards.

This sophisticated concept had been countenanced, oddly
enough, by Akhenaton's father, Amenhotep III, the last great
ruler of the Eighteenth Dynasty, the first part of the New
Kingdom.   It was foreign to Egyptian religious thinking, but
probably considered harmless, embraced by very few.   But
when Akhenaton took it up, he went the whole way, repudiating
Amon-Re, the established god of Thebes, and changing his
name from Amenhotep IV to Akhenaton.   This was like turning
his back on the whole empire and on the imposing roster of
gods and goddesses whose forms and faces had long been familiar to Egyptians.   When he became pharaoh he struck out
the name of Amon wherever he could, neglecting the old temples and putting money and effort into the creation of altars
to Aton.

Naturally this caused commotion in priestly circles.   We
must bear in mind that the city of Thebes was the most important city in Egypt and was fast becoming the most renowned
in the Mediterranean world.   Boats from Thebes went down
the Nile and out into the sea to Crete.   They touched at Phoenician ports in Asia Minor.   They ventured down to ports on
the Red Sea coast.   Caravans may have gone as far as Mesopotamia.   The priests of Amon were well-known because their

political and economic power was something to reckon with.

If a governor of an Egyptian province wanted to put up a building, he had to consult an overseer of works—who was a priest. When the pharaoh wanted to organize a trading expedition he did it under the auspices of a god and he left the details to someone who could propitiate that god—a priest. If a farmer got into a dispute over his land, or had irrigation problems, or had trouble with his taxes, he sought help from the local scribe—who was undoubtedly a priest.

Thus Egypt at the end of the Middle Kingdom was served by a complex priestly bureaucracy. Since religion and economy were so closely linked, the priest was a key man in civil matters,

on his way to becoming indispensable. As a class, the priests, by controlling the purse strings of the country, could threaten the power of the pharaoh.

Akhenaton, who was sixteen or seventeen when he ascended the throne, did not struggle long with the priestly establishment. He simply walked out. Imbued with his vision of Aton, disillusioned by the corruption which was hardening the minds of his people, he departed like the Pied Piper, taking a band of devoted believers with him. He chose a site about three hundred miles down river from Thebes, carefully marking out the limits of his new city.

Akhetaton, or Amarna, as it is called today, was one of the first planned cities in existence. Like Washington, D.C., or Brasilia, Brazil's new capital built in the jungle, Amarna rose from the banks of the Nile on a spot where no town or village had been before.

It must have been a beautiful place. Although virtually nothing is left of Amarna today, archaeologists have found remains of several temples, three palaces, and several large buildings. We know that the city had straight, parallel streets with square intersections at the corners. There was a planned workmen's quarter. Fine terraced houses mingled with simpler dwellings. From pictures in tombs we can get a fairly good impression of the layout of the city, with its abundant flowers, pools, and parks—a dream city brought to reality by a king whose artistic sensibilities were strong.

Akhenaton, young as he was, must have had great personal magnetism to be able to convince his followers of his mission. We know little about his background, but historians suspect that he may not even have been pure Egyptian. His mother, Queen Tiy, had been a court favorite whom his father had elevated to the rank of royal consort. Some writers claim that she was a princess from the country of the Mitanni, north of Palestine; others write her off as a "nobody." At any rate, Tiy soon became somebody and her influence over both her husband and

This is a painted limestone bust of Nefertiti. State Museum of Berlin.

her son was strong. She remained a determined woman.

She supported her son in his break with convention, coming to Amarna with him to live in the palace. As for the others who came—who were they? Men and women from all ranks of society, probably; people to whom the achieving of a new kind of life was important. Many were artists, sculptors, or poets of real ability. In their break with tradition they achieved a new freedom in art. The stiffness of the conventional forms relaxed. Rigid figures began to unbend and take on a pleasing familiarity. We see pictures of Akhenaton and his queen enjoying life with their children, not as gods but as human beings, doing the things ordinary people do.

Amarna art tells us a great deal about new concepts in this period. Sweeping lines and free-form curves began to suggest emphasis on individuality, although, to be sure, fluidity and grace were not lacking in Egyptian art before the Amarna period.

Sculptors began to produce realistic human figures. Queen Tiy is an individual, perhaps not a likeable one. Queen Nefertiti, whose sculptured head ranks as one of the great art works of the world, speaks to us from a distance of 3,350 years in a way that the impassive Egyptian portraits cannot. In the ruins of Amarna archaeologists have found the remains of at least one sculptor's studio, which could well have been one of many in a school of "modern art" enjoying the patronage of the king.

Akhenaton himself expressed his ecstasy in poetry, notably a long hymn to Aton, "sole god, whose powers no other possesseth." The mood is very like that of our Psalm 104, and it carries out the idea of oneness to the very beginning of things:

Thou didst create the earth according to thy heart
While thou wast alone.

Other poetry of the times has the same note of lyric ecstacy. The pompous superlatives offered to the old-time gods had given way to an outpouring of wonder, as though the poets had just discovered the amazing life force descending from the sky.

But the ideal community at Amarna, like many to follow in later history, was doomed to failure. Its leader, a man who grasped life's subtleties, completely missed its hard facts. While the inspired nonconformist insisted that his god took care of the least of people, Egyptian farmers were being grievously taxed by the Amon priests. While the believer in One God for One World promised that Aton's rays would shine protectively on everybody, Egyptian outposts in Syria were being seriously harassed by Egypt's old enemies the Hittites.

Akhenaton was a man ahead of his time. He encouraged a trend in art that included completely original elements. His religious beliefs sparked the first major effort of a group of people to live according to a principle which was different from the prevailing beliefs.

Acknowledging the sun as the generating force of mankind may have worked for a few imaginative people. But without the supportive evidence of images and legends such worship was incomprehensible to the rank and file. Egyptians needed their myths. The Greeks, whose civilization came after them, and the Romans, who followed, would also seek reassurance from a divine family of gods and goddesses.

The community at Amarna survived through Akhenaton's reign of seventeen years. When he died, it died also. His son-in-law, Tut-ankh-aton, a mere boy when he ascended the throne, soon fell into the hands of the Theban priests, waiting for this moment to seize the power. He was persuaded to change his name to Tut-ankh-*amon* and move his capital back to Thebes. After his short reign, a priest named Ay, one of Aton's loudest supporters, married one of the princesses and took over the power, swerving his allegience to Amon. But Ay was an old man. When death caught up with him he was followed by an able general, Horemhab, who turned out to be both hard working and politically astute. With all the vigor

Colossal statue of Ramses II supports part of the wall of a Nubian Temple.

and ruthlessness Akhenaton had lacked, he settled the turbulent priests, sent troops to aid the colonies in Syria, and had Aton's name scratched from the monuments. The central government was once more in strong hands.

Amarna became deserted. Perhaps a few stragglers—artists, writers, and dreamers—hung on in the silent city, hoping to keep their blessed fellowship alive. It is more likely that they were chased out by the vindictive and now infuriated Amon priests. At any rate, houses, temples, art studios were soon vacant. The gardens withered and died. Amarna, city of the sun, was left to the night-prowlers.

The old order was changing. Egypt would never again be

a small, self-contained unit.   The great pharaohs, Ramses I,
Ramses II, and Ramses III, who founded a new dynasty and
ushered in the prosperous times of her New Kingdom, would
be hard-headed and aggressive.   Egypt's borders would extend
from northern Syria to Nubia.   Amarna art styles may have
brought a new realism, but their charm lay in their spontaneity,
which later artists failed to grasp.   Art never went back to the
stately simplicity of former times.   Gradually painting took on
a sort of gaudy overstatement, proclaiming the wealth of an
important nation.

Nevertheless, the period stands out in the philosophical history of man as one of the first fumbling efforts to see beyond
the literal truth.   The disk, with its reaching-down rays which
never quite touch the earth or its people, reminds us that a
man's reach must exceed his grasp—perhaps for a long time
to come.

Hymn to Aton

Bright is the earth when thou risest in the horizon.
When thou shinest as Aton by day
Thou drivest away the darkness.
When thou sendest forth thy rays
The Two Lands are in daily festivity.
Awake and standing on their feet
When thou hast raised them up.
Their limbs bathed, they take their clothing,
Their arms uplifted in adoration to thy dawning
Then in all the world they do their work.

How manifold are thy works!
They are hidden from before us,
O sole God, whose powers no other possesseth.
Thou didst create the earth according to thy heart
While thou wast alone:
Men, all cattle, large and small,
All that go upon the earth,

That go about on their feet:
All that are on high
That fly with wings.
The foreign countries, Syria and Kush,
The land of Egypt,
Thou settest every man in his place. . . .

Psalm 104

He appointed the moon for seasons:
  the sun knoweth his going down.
Thou makest darkness and it is night:
  wherein all the beasts of the forest do creep forth. . . .
The sun ariseth, they gather themselves together;
  and lay them down in their dens.
Man goeth forth unto his work
  and to his labor until evening.

O Lord, how manifold are thy works!
  in wisdom thou hast made them all:
  the earth is full of thy riches.
So is this great and wide sea,
Wherein are things creeping innumerable
  with small and great beasts.
Thou hidest thy face, they are troubled:
  thou takest away their breath,
  they die, and return to dust.
Thou sendest forth thy spirit, they are created:
  and thou renewest the face of the earth.

I will sing to the Lord as long as I live:
  I will sing to praise my God while I have any being.
  Bless thou the Lord, O my soul. Praise ye the Lord.

chapter 12

EGYPT AND THE MEDITERRANEAN

"With a cargo of Ivory, and apes,
    and peacocks,
Sandalwood and cedarwood,
    and sweet white wine."

John Masefield, *Cargoes.*

"I, Sinuhe, a courtier, a prince
and a noble, keeper of the seal of the King of Lower Egypt,
judge and district governor in the land of the Bedouins, and
friend of the ruler, write thus: I am a friend of King Sesostris
and servant of his gracious queen. . . ."

Thus the writer of this letter, in exile somewhere in Syria,
addresses the Pharaoh and begs to be allowed to return.
Sinuhe, now old and honored among his Bedouin friends, was
admittedly homesick. He had traveled far and had seen strange
things, but he wished to die in his native land of Egypt.

The pharaoh, Sesostris, would have been hard-hearted indeed
if he had not let Sinuhe return. The circumstances of his
leaving were obscure. Some say that as a young soldier he had
been implicated in an assassination plot; he had grown fearful

and had sneaked across Egypt's northeast border. But that was years ago and the affair had blown over.   Furthermore, Sinuhe had made good in the wilderness.   He'd learned a lot, seen a lot, and had undoubtedly accumulated some wealth.   A grateful tribal chieftain had given him extensive property in a land with the fairytale-sounding name of Yaa.   It would have been foolish to banish him forever.

Sesostris sent messengers with letters urging Sinuhe to come back with all haste: "The Pharaoh Sesostris the Divine, the Keeper of Upper and Lower Egypt, may he live forever, commands thus: To my courtier Sinuhe, you have journeyed through foreign lands. . . . Return now to Egypt where you may . . . kiss the soil of the Big Twin Gates, and may rejoice in the company of your friends at the palace."   He went on to promise

Flute player accompanies dancing girls, in a fresco of a court scene. British Museum.

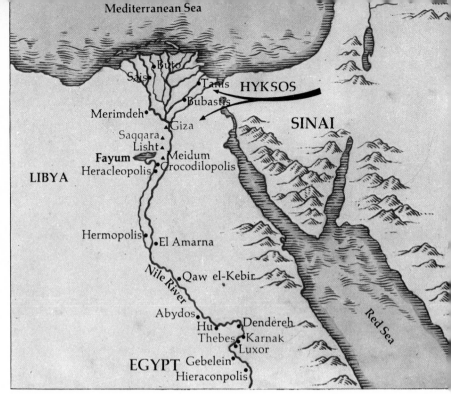

Many invaders of Egypt crossed the Sinai Desert, following the route of the Hyksos.

an Egyptian burial: "Syrians will not accompany you to your grave, nor will you be wrapped in sheepskin."

After further exchange of grandiose sentiments, Sinuhe arrived at the court of Thebes and prostrated himself in the dust before the King. He must have cut quite a figure in his striped Bedouin turban. Stories about his heroic exploits in a little-known land had preceded him and he was treated like a visiting celebrity: "My hair was curled. I was cleansed from the desert sand. I was clad in a robe of byssus linen and had a bed to sleep on."

The story ends happily. The expatriate, world traveler, and loyal Egyptian is promised a funeral which exceeds his wildest hopes—a gold-covered sarcophagus and a tomb beside that of the royal children.

Sir Alan Gardiner, the great British linguistics expert, regards this Middle Kingdom story of Sinuhe as Egypt's great epic. It certainly has the qualities of adventure, exotic background,

142

and a hero whose exploits command respect. His banishment and his magnanimous pardon by the Pharaoh simply add to his appeal.

But the significant thing about the story is its purely Egyptian character. During the Middle Kingdom the country was just beginning to be aware of the fact that she had neighbors. The Egyptians wanted to know more about the people who roved the deserts beyond her borders. The fact that the repentent wayfarer left his own family and came home to die is also interesting. The Pharaoh's first thought was to assure Sinuhe that his mummy would receive full rites, that it would not be contaminated by a sheepskin (horrifying thought to an Egyptian!). His afterlife was assured.

Egyptians were never to be explorers like the Cretans or the Phoenicians, whose boats traveled thousands of miles across the sea, some think as far as the coasts of North and South America. They had not the restlessness of the Norsemen, to whom a vast ocean was a challenge. What need to explore, or even to trade, if you had everything you wanted at home? With his house and garden, his family and his perpetual sunshine, plying the river in his little boat, what more could the Egyptian want?

There were, of course, exceptions. Spasmodic trading expeditions, usually sponsored by the government, ventured out into the Mediterranean. A few caravans trekked across the desert to the east. Several expeditions went to Punt, farther down the coast, no one knows exactly where.

In the Mediterranean it was inevitable that Egypt should come into contact with her nearest neighbors, the cities on the coast of Syria and Palestine. She also had some knowledge of Mycenaean Greece. Egyptian scarabs have turned up in Mycenaean tombs; vases of obviously Mycenaean design have appeared in Egyptian tombs. Yet Egypt probably played host to seagoing nations far more often than she visited their shores. Conscious of her separateness and superiority, she confined herself to a few well-organized expeditions.

(Above Left.) Ancient Egyptians slept on wooden headrests like this one in the shape of a hare. British Museum. (Above Right.) The prince in this statue appears stiff and dignified. Louvre. (Below.) This ornament of embossed gold shows the goddess Ma'at. Museum of Cairo. (Far Right.) Boats, such as this painted wooden model, were commonly used for Nile excursions. Louvre.

One of the high points of Herodotus' visit to Egypt in 470 B.C. was coming to a temple-tomb near Lake Moeris, part of which was a complex set of corridors and chambers. He was not allowed to visit the burial chamber, but he reports, with some awe, that the place had "3,000 rooms." He called it a labyrinth, which in Greek means corridor, or maze, but has come to stand ever since for a place of great complexity.

Everyone knows the Greek legend. A young man named Theseus came to Crete and slew the Minotaur, the sinister half man, half bull, who lived in the Labyrinth. Theseus threaded

his way through the maze with a spool given him by Ariadne, daughter of King Minos. With this legend as part of his heritage, Herodotus, when viewing this complex Egyptian temple, naturally gave it the name "labyrinth."

During the prosperous days of the New Kingdom, Egyptian ships ventured farther and farther north in the Mediterranean. By this time they had a stockpile of goods to exchange for raw materials—papyrus, unguents, jewelry, cleverly fashioned tools and weapons. In Lebanon they found the precious cedar wood, which they used to build their seagoing ships. There was little timber in Egypt. As trade expanded, so did knowledge of geography and language. Travelers ventured east as far as Mesopotamia, where another great river culture, Babylonia, was beginning to sink into a decline. Young scribes, in addition to mastering hieroglyphic writing, were made to learn the cuneiform script of the Babylonians. This system of stiff, vertical, wedge-shaped characters pressed into clay tablets was quite different from the colorful, complicated hieroglyphs.

There is a story concerning a sea captain named Wenamon, commissioned to buy cedars from Lebanon for a Theban priest. He not only lost his credentials en route, but was robbed of the small amount of silver he'd been given to make his purchase. When he showed up empty-handed in the harbor at Byblos, Zakar-Baal, the Phoenician king, laughed at him in scorn. Who did Wenamon think he was, appearing with no money, no fine fleet of ships, begging for timber?

Fortunately Wenamon carried a small wooden statue of Amon, called Amon-of-the-Ways (i.e., Seas), to insure safe voyage—a sort of St. Christopher medal. He showed it to Zakar-Baal and gave him a promise to pay. The Phoenician ruler finally gave Wenamon his timber on credit and let him go.

This is a story from Egypt's Intermediate Period. Even in this period of decline, her reputation for wealth was well known. The Phoenician king simply would not believe that one of her envoys could be in such dire straits—yet the Theban god Amon was familiar to him and apparently swayed his decision.

Imports weren't all in the form of goods; they sometimes consisted of people. In the luxurious days of the New Kingdom, "dancing girls" appeared in court, brought from the East, exotic creatures whose sinuous acrobatics and backbends add a note of gaiety to some of the tomb paintings. A pharaoh often imported a dusky beauty to his harem. Why not? The lady was an adornment and her presence could insure happy relations with some outlying country.

Slaves appeared, too, in the wake of successfully waged wars, for relations with neighbors weren't always peaceful. Statues of slaves captured in battle are unmistakable, with their looks of terror or abject submission. They are quite a contrast to the dignified, stylized Egyptians.

For almost two thousand years the civilization which had come into being and prospered along the banks of the Nile had nothing to fear from invaders because her deserts and her cataracts kept her seemingly impregnable. During that period far to the east in Mesopotamia, two great empires rose and fell again, almost contemporaneous with Egypt's two great periods of strength, the Old and the Middle Kingdom.

The fatal thing inevitably happened. Under a succession of weak pharaohs in the Middle Kingdom, Egypt as she had in the past became divided against herself. This time the country was wide open to a wandering horde that surged across the Sinai Peninsula and simply took over.

No one knows exactly who the invaders were or where they had come from. The Egyptians called them the Hyksos; we often call them the Shepherd Kings. They were apparently nomads who had pillaged Babylon and pressed on through Syria, gathering strength as they picked up more and more followers. A large number of Canaanites joined them just before they reached Egypt.

The takeover was easy. The Hyksos had picked up a number of good ideas in their wanderings. One of them was the usefulness of the horse in warfare. They thundered into the startled villages in their horse-drawn chariots, terrifying people.

Egypt fell to the Hyksos in 1720 B.C. The new rulers promptly established their capital at the city of Avaris, in the Delta. Fortunately they did not venture much farther south; they knew better than to try to spread themselves thin along the length of the Nile. Thus the land was split again into two kingdoms of unequal strength, the South having to answer to the North in all respects.[1]

Contrary to some reports, the Hyksos were not a cruel people. They were undoubtedly arrogant. When the chance came, Egypt struck back. During their many long years of occupation, they did learn the skillful use of the horse and chariot. In about 1590 B.C., a man named Ahmose from Upper Egypt succeeded in throwing the Hyksos back. His brother, Khamose, completed the job, driving Apophis III, the last of the Hyksos kings, across the border.

[1] The history of the Hyksos period is still unclear. We are not sure just who the Hyksos were nor when they arrived in Egypt. Hyksos peoples may have been moving into the Delta in the Twelfth Dynasty of the Middle Kingdom. Some Hyksos persons appear to have risen to important positions under Egyptian kings. At any rate later (in the Second Intermediate Period, at a time when the country was weakened) they were able to gain dominance over Lower Egypt. This move may have been accompanied by an influx of Hyksos from Palestine. The Hyksos rulers appear to have tried to become Egyptians, taking Egyptian names and titles. A Hyksos city is now being excavated in Egypt, therefore we should presently know a great deal more about these peoples.

Egypt's time of troubles was over.   Proudly Ahmose put on the double crown and assumed the symbolic crook and flail of Upper and Lower Egypt. But something new had been added. The horse, instrument of Egypt's downfall, had become her salvation.

Although the Hyksos left no other mark on Egypt, they did leave the door ajar for other visitors, not always welcome. Most historians conclude that the Hebrew migration into Egypt took place at the end of the Hyksos rule, or just after they had departed.   Joseph and his brothers were assigned a special place, Goshen, not far from the Hyksos capital at Avaris.[1] Here they existed as a tightly knit unit, resenting their hosts, who undoubtedly grew less and less kindly as time wore on. Dislike of the settlers in the east Delta hardened into snobbery. Egyptians "might not eat bread with the Hebrews," we are told in Genesis.

Thus a royal "favor" withered away into enslavement—from the Hebrew vantage point at least.   "And the Egyptians made the Children of Israel to serve with rigor," the Book of Exodus tells us.   "And they made their lives bitter with hard bondage, in mortar and in brick, and in all manner of service in the field."   Even before this, Exodus tells us, the Pharaoh had tried to exterminate all Hebrew baby boys by urging midwives to do away with them discreetly at birth.   But the midwives had refused, explaining that Hebrew women were "lively," and quite able to bear their children alone.   Rather than lose their jobs, midwives remained loyal to their Hebrew patients.

Egyptians left no records of the departure of the Israelites across the Red Sea swampland.   It was probably not as dramatic as represented in Exodus.   As the Hebrews grew more restive, the Egyptians grew more apprehensive about the hardy, emotional group in Goshen, who had never known a permanent home.   To the restrained Egyptians, whose homeland, from

[1] The exact location of the Land of Goshen has not been determined.

This comical clay hippo, a household ornament,
is decorated with swamp plants. Louvre.

time immemorial, had been neatly mapped out by a river, all
foreigners, whether they came as conquerors or conquered, were
inferior; only Egyptians were "men."

No one knows for sure when Moses led his people out of
Egypt. A series of emigrations took place between 1400 and
1300 B.C., and the land of Goshen was cleared.

Invaders would come to Egypt, both from the East and from
the sea, and they would stay. But for the moment, at least,
Egyptian life could proceed according to Egyptian pattern.

And the Hebrews were glad to be on the move once more.
The early tribal name may have been *Habiru,* or wanderer.
Continuing search was to be their pattern for a number of
years. Placing their faith in their god, Yahweh, they drifted
in family units, east, then north—ever onward toward the
Promised Land, little realizing that there, under the leadership
of their great prophets, they would find their spiritual home.
Their greatness was yet to come.[1]

[1] The entire history of the Hebrews in Egypt is problematical. The dates of their entry
and departure, as well as the nature of these events, are uncertain. The biblical narrative
cannot be taken as absolute fact, nor can the identification of the Hebrews with the
Habiru.

The ruins of the funeral temple of Ramses the Great at Thebes are surrounded by crumbling shops and houses.

chapter 13

RAMSES THE GREAT

"I myself am more divine than any I see."

Margaret Fuller,
Letter to Ralph Waldo Emerson, March 1, 1838.

I met a traveler from an antique land
Who said: Two vast and trunkless legs of stone
Stand in the desert . . . Near them on the sand
Half sunk, a shattered visage lies, whose frown
And wrinkled lip, the sneer of cold command
Tell that its sculptor well those passions read
Which yet survive, stamped on these lifeless things,
The hand that mocked them and the hand that fed:
And on the pedestal these words appear:
"My name is Ozymandias, king of kings;
Look on my works, ye mighty, and despair!"
Nothing beside remains. Round the decay
Of the colossal wreck, boundless and bare,
The lone and level sands stretch far away.

Percy Bysshe Shelley, *Ozymandias*.

THE broken statue which
Shelley refers to in his ironic sonnet is that of the Nineteenth
Dynasty pharaoh Ramses II, called Ramses the Great. Considering his accomplishments, he might better have been called
Ramses the Most. Compared with other rulers, he had the
most land; Egypt's boundaries during his reign were extended
from Nubia to Asia Minor. He had the most money; tributes
poured in from vassal states. He had the most statues; a compulsive interest in self-duplication kept his sculptors busy creating likenesses of Ramses, most of them outsize, all over Egypt.

It is doubtful, though, that Shelley ever saw this enormous
statue, which lies broken on the desert at Thebes. If he did,
he misinterpreted the expression on its face in the light of his
own romantic generation. The lips aren't twisted; the face

has no frown, and certainly no "sneer of cold command." No Egyptian sculptor would have dreamed of representing a person, much less a pharaoh, in such terms. The King's visage, like those in all Egyptian art, has a calm, almost oriental expression of dignity. It does not need to frown. The fact that it sits ignominiously on the sand, its royal beard cut off and lying a few feet from its huge body, does not seem to disturb it in the least.

Ramses the Great could boast a strong ancestry. His grandfather, Ramses I, was a general, a man of practical affairs, founder of the Nineteenth Dynasty. The royal blood, which had petered out with Tutankhamon, had been given a much-needed transfusion.

His energy knew no bounds. He spent his whole career either fighting or erecting colossal reminders of the greatness of Egypt, the might of Amon, and the eternal glory of himself.

"Crown him king, so that I may see his beauty while I am still alive," Ramses' father, Seti, had said of his son. And so Ramses ascended the throne as a young man. He was to reign for sixty-seven years.

He immediately put his mind to strengthening his vast empire. Troubles in Syria and Palestine had plagued pharaohs for generations. The powerful Hittites now controlled Mesopotamia and continued to harry the northern borders of Syria. In the fifth year of his reign Ramses assembled a large army, its four divisions each carrying the name of a god, and Ramses himself heading up the division of Amon. His destination was Kadesh, a Hittite stronghold on the Orontes River.

The march took almost a month. When the soldiers approached they took up positions on a hill overlooking the city. It was certainly well fortified, with its two moats and flanking river. But as the men looked they couldn't see a living soul. No sound, no movement—not even lookouts posted on the battlements. This was odd. Was the place deserted? Had the Hittites retreated?

Cautiously Ramses advanced with his crack Amon division. At this point two men were brought before him, who claimed to be deserters from the Hittite army. Muwatallis, the Hittite king, they said, had retreated to the northwest.

Ramses should have known better, but he fell right into the trap. He pushed on with his division, impatient to find Muwatallis, leaving others to guard the southern approaches to the fortress. They were just getting ready to camp for the night when he learned the truth: Muwatallis and a formidable army were hiding inside the fortress.

Muwatallis now had the Egyptians just where he wanted them—three groups to the south and his royal prey, Ramses, helpless on the north. Furiously he descended on one of the divisions, scattering the troops. Then he moved toward the division of Amon.

Ramses hastily dispatched a messenger to summon aid. Whether or not any soldiers came to his assistance has never been made precisely clear because of his own account of the battle—which has a certain dash. It appears that, abandoned by his army, Ramses drove his own chariot against some 25,000 chariots of the Hittites. "They were three men to a pair of horses," he laments, "whereas there was no captain with me, no driver, no shieldbearer." During the combat he prayed to Amon: "What ails thee, my father Amon? . . . Have I not made for thee many monuments and temples with my booty?" He then trampled the Hittites under his chariot and drove the rest of them into the Orontes River, where they were drowned.

Here is one of the most remarkable cases of divine intervention on record. The great pharaoh's subjects may have bought the story as they saw it engraved in detail on the walls of Ramses' temple. History has taken a more skeptical view, especially after a Hittite account of the same battle turned up recently, reporting a sweeping victory over the vile Egyptians.

The truth is that the battle ended in a draw. The Egyptians never occupied Kadesh. After years of inconclusive bickering,

The colossal and tiny statues guard the entrance to the temple of Ramses the Great at Abu Simbel.

both sides agreed to respect a common border between their countries. They sealed a treaty of mutual aid. Muwatallis gave Ramses one of his daughters for a wife and she was escorted by a royal guard back to Egypt. She was to be in good company. In addition to his queen, Nefertari, Ramses is said to have married his mother and three of his daughters and to have sired from 100 to 150 children. His self-perpetuation could be safely assured.

Ramses now turned his attention to building. As single-minded in his creation of public monuments as he was in war, he built temples, obelisks, statues, all inscribed with his name and records of his deeds. He added a court to the great temple of Amenhotep III at Thebes. His own mortuary temple on the west bank of the river was a sprawling affair, called the Ramesseum by the Greeks, the "thinking place of Ramses the Great." The sixty-foot statue in front proclaims the owner. Two temples built into the cliffs at Abu Simbel, at the Fifth

Cataract of the Nile, marked the southernmost limits of the empire. The larger belongs to Ramses (who else?); the smaller to Queen Nefertari, and was dedicated to the goddess Hathor.

It was to the temple complex at Karnak that Ramses added his most ambitious work. The celebrated Hypostyle Hall is today, next to the pyramids, one of the great marvels in Egypt. Here again, Ramses thought big. The seventy-eight-foot columns in the central hall are so thick that one hundred people could stand comfortably on the top of one of them. Yet the architect of this hall must have been a genius with an eye for balance and unity. The effect of the mass is not oppressive. Murals in blue and red on walls and columns relieve the long lines of stonework. The famous clerestory windows at the top let in light in long shafts.

Ramses' zeal for building suggests that he may be the pharaoh under whose reign the Hebrews, led by Moses, made their famous departure from Egypt. We have already mentioned the Hebrew miseries described in the Book of Exodus. One verse specifically mentions the place-name of Ramses: "And they built for Pharaoh treasure cities [probably garrisons or outposts] Pithom and Raamses."

No one knows where these places were, but we do know that Ramses the Great built a temple in this region, and the usual colossus to himself. He also set up a number of small villages with storehouses for equipment in his Syrian campaigns. He could very well have used cheap local labor. Who would have been more convenient than the teeming, unwanted Hebrews?

Moses had been brought up at court. As the adopted son of an Egyptian princess, he was given a good education at the College of Heliopolis in the Delta, not too far from Goshen. Outwardly he was probably not much different from most Egyptian boys—clean-shaven, with short dark hair and his loose white linen garment to his knees. But in background and in lineage as well as temperament he was different; in his veins ran the blood of the sons of Abraham. Certainly as he grew older he must have felt closer to his own kinsmen and sensed their unrest. Brawls between Egyptians and Hebrews were common. Exodus reports that to protect a Hebrew, Moses became involved in a fight with an Egyptian, whom he killed and buried in the sand. After several years of hiding, a burning sense of injustice prodded him to go back to lead one sector of the great migration of the Israelites across the Isthmus of Suez toward the Promised Land.[1]

All this could have taken place at the end of the reign of Ramses the Great, or his successor, Merneptah. As the Pharaoh grew older, wealthier, fatter, his energetic efforts declined. He lived the latter part of his life in self-indulgence and died when he was ninety. The long attenuated reign was not healthy for the country, already beginning to be jolted by wars, social dissent, and affluence.

At the temple of Ramses at Abu Simbel, four huge seated statues of the Pharaoh guard the entrance. The Pharaoh is surrounded by his family in miniature figures reaching no higher than his knees. Nearby is the temple of Nefertari, his queen. Both temples, carved from living rock, recently underwent a massive moving operation to a site above their original location, in order to protect them from the waters of the Aswan High Dam flooding the area. A team of UNESCO engineers worked for four years, at a cost of $40 million, moving some 2,000 thirty-ton blocks of stone.

With the cooperation of the world, the Pharaoh is now 214 feet above where he used to sit. Ramses (all four of him) will now look down on a large lake, from the most highly placed position in Egypt.

The Pharaoh will be pleased.

---

[1] If the Exodus is dated to Ramses II or Merneptah, it took place later than the date 1400–1300 B.C. sometimes given. Accounts of Moses do not appear in Egyptian records.

These graceful figures prepare to make oil out of the lotus blossom.
Museum of Turin.

chapter 14

THE LEGACY OF EGYPT

"The earth sighed as it turned on its course; the shadow of night crept gradually along the Mediterranean, and Asia was left in darkness. . . . Triumph had passed from Greece and wisdom from Egypt, but with the coming of night they seemed to regain their lost honors, and the land that was soon to be called Holy prepared in the dark its precious burden."

Thornton Wilder, *The Woman of Andros.*

THE sixty-seven-year reign of Ramses the Great was certainly one of the most grandiose in history. Like a skyrocket he zoomed over the Mediterranean world, then fizzed and went out. After he died in 1223 B.C., Egypt, despite her large empire and her enormous resources of wealth, was never the same again.

The reasons are numerous. The simplest have to do with geography. All the neat little barriers, which had kept Egypt snug and aloof for centuries, were now down, and had become, in fact, gateways. The campaigns in Syria had opened up a passage across the Sinai Peninsula, making two-way traffic possible. Even the Nile cataracts were no longer serious deterrents; portage around them was possible. The vast, arid stretch of western desert failed to keep out invaders from Libya who drifted in and eventually took over after the weak successors of Ramses II (called Ramessids) had died out.   They established a capital at Bubastis, setting up their own royal line, the Twenty-second Dynasty.

But the most wide open of all the floodgates was the Mediterranean.   Little by little, Egypt's cities were beginning to be harried by "peoples from the sea."[1]   Ships from Sidon and Tyre were also to be reckoned with; Phoenicia's great maritime empire was reaching its height.

With the great Israelite migrations, which began at the end of the reign of Ramses the Great, it seemed as though the whole world was on the move, spurred on by unrest, by a search for better land, or by fear of stronger neighbors.

Egypt, with her succession of weak pharaohs, could do little more than watch and weakly defend herself.   The old patterns were changing; the old rules no longer held.   In a shifting, expanding world she was wide open for invaders.

The new generation of attackers had their secret weapon—iron.   Its discovery and use is credited to the Hittites, who converted it into weapons more accurate, more deadly than any before.   But it was not so much the Hittites' weapons but Egypt's internal weakness, caused by a variety of conditions, that brought about her downfall.

The Assyrians, with a completely mechanized, admirably disciplined army, sacked Thebes in 661 B.C. and all but demolished it.   Then came the Persians, deadliest of all enemies and the strongest.   The Persian domination lasted for various periods over approximately 130 years.   Eventually they bowed in turn to the tidal wave of Greeks, which threatened to inundate not only Egypt, but the whole world.

When Alexander the Great of Macedonia took over Egypt in 331 B.C., he encountered little opposition.   In fact, he was hailed as "liberator."   Almost as good a diplomat as he was

---

[1] The "Peoples from the Sea" is a general term used to refer to various peoples on the move who threatened not only Egypt but all countries which ringed the Mediterranean.

Royal figure made of basalt may be either a pharaoh of the 25th Dynasty or a Ptolemy living about the time of Alexander.   Louvre.

a warrior, he was careful to observe Egyptian ways and respect her customs. He was shrewd enough to have himself crowned pharaoh, the "divine son of Amon," after first obtaining the priest's divine seal of approval.

On the far-off Libyan desert oasis of Siwa was a small temple of Amon. With a few chosen followers Alexander proceeded to this place, where he was met by the priest, who came out hailing him as the son of god.

The rest was easy. All Alexander needed to do now was to follow the priestly rites and receive the final blessing of Amon. The Egyptians, weary of foreign invaders, were glad to accept him on these terms.

Amon, incidentally, had strange companions. He had gotten on astonishingly well as Amon-Re ever since the end of the Eighteenth Dynasty, and his prestige was known all over the world. Now he would be worshipped as Zeus-Amon. Later on, after the Greeks departed, he would become Jupiter-Amon in deference to the new Roman rulers.

In a curious way, Amon's name became associated with one of our commonest modern cleaning agents. Smoke from the camel dung fires in the temples used to leave a sooty deposit on the ceilings, which turned into crystals the Romans called *sal ammoniac,* or salt of Amon. The gas obtained from these crystals eventually became known as ammonia.

As ruler of Egypt, Alexander's greatest move had been to establish his city. He chose the site carefully, at the mouth of the westernmost branch of the Nile, where the configuration of coastland provided for two harbors. He called it Alexandria. A Greek architect, Dinocrates, from the Isle of Rhodes, laid out the city in broad streets, some of them a hundred feet wide and colonnaded to protect people from the sun. With its neat right-angled crossings and white buildings it resembled a modern city. It was to become great—one of the foremost trade centers of the world and the capital of Ptolemaic Egypt.

Alexander never lived to see the city's greatness. He died

in Babylon of fever in 323 B.C., returning from his eastern campaign. He was only thirty-three years old. Legend has it that his body was embalmed in honey and returned to Memphis, then to Alexandria, where it now rests.

The governorship of Egypt fell to a Greek general named Ptolemy, one of Alexander's most capable aides. Some historians say that he seized it, some that Alexander gave it to him. Let's say that Ptolemy was there when countries were being parceled out after the emperor's death. He ruled Egypt wisely and his line lasted for three centuries, all taking the kingly name of Ptolemy. Early in his reign he was given the epithet Soter, "the Savior," and it is as Ptolemy Soter that he is known to history.

Alexandria became a crossroads. Migrating Jews, Greeks, and Egyptians created a ferment of new ideas, new scientific and philosophical works, new customs. It began to attract the best minds of the rapidly expanding world.

The early Ptolemies were dedicated patrons of learning. When Aristotle died, leaving his library to Ptolemy Soter, it was given to the city of Alexandria and formed the nucleus of the great Alexandrian Library, which eventually boasted some 400,000 volumes. The Mouseion (museum), a temple to the muses, was in reality a working place for the thousands of scholars who came to use the library. In its greatest period this large gathering place accommodated as many as 14,000 scholars. Here Euclid, the Greek mathematician, expounded his theories of geometry, and a geographer named Eratosthenes measured the circumference of the earth. Manetho, chronicler of Egypt, wrote his history here. A man named Heron invented the first successful steam engine. It was considered an interesting toy and forgotten. (It remained for Watt and Fulton to invent it all over again, some 2,000 years later.)

What kindled the information explosion and made Alexandria such an exciting place to live was the general atmosphere of lively inquiry. The air fairly crackled with it, as astronomers,

In the late period of Egyptian art, the sunken reliefs are dramatically etched by their own shadows. British Museum.

technologists, philosophers, and theologians jostled one another in the streets. Greeks from Athens came to learn from the Egyptians as well as to share their own learning with others. Jews were given complete freedom to worship. In fact, the first translation of the Old Testament from Hebrew to Greek was commissioned at Alexandria. It was called the Septuagint, or the "work of seventy scholars."

A curious pseudo-science that grew up in Alexandria was that of alchemy. This was the belief, or rather the wishful hope, that the nature of metals could be changed—specifically that lead could be turned into gold. Scholars pursued this dream well into medieval times. The Greeks called it *Khemia,* the Egyptian science. (Its root goes back to an ancient Egyptian word, *kemet,* meaning "the Black Land.") It traveled a long way to become the root of our modern word *chemistry.*[1]

[1]The Egyptians called their country "The Black Land" in contrast to the desert or "Red Land" because the fertile soil of Egypt is almost black in color.

Because of the Greek infiltration many Egyptian names changed to Greek, their originals lost or distorted. The origin of the word for Egypt is itself obscure. The Greeks probably took it from one of the names of the old capital of Memphis— Huk-ka-ptah, "the temple of the spirit of Ptah," which they mispronounced as Aegyptos.

Sometimes old names persisted along with the new, and both are still used, depending on the taste or whim of the historian. The Old Kingdom pharaohs Khufu (Cheops) and Khafre (Chephren) have been trailing their Greek names for centuries and will probably never get rid of them.

The royal palace at Alexandria occupied the southeast corner of the Great Harbor. A flight of steps led to the water of a smaller inlet called the Royal Harbor. Here the royal visitors embarked and disembarked again for the Mediterranean.

Ships going out at night would have no fear of the treacherous reefs blocking the two harbors because they followed beams from a giant lighthouse five hundred feet high, which cast its light for seventy miles.

This architectural and technical wonder stood on an island called Pharos, commanding the Great Harbor. It was four stories high, the bottom being square, windowed, and containing (it is reported) three hundred rooms. The second story, octagonal in shape, was reached by a spiral stairway, coiling through the middle to a third story, which was circular. Above this was the lantern, in reality a huge bonfire kindled each night. A statue of Poseidon, Greek god of the sea, was here too, and another statue, whose moving finger followed the course of the sun. Still another statue was reported to bellow out an alarm as soon as an enemy ship appeared in the harbor.

The existence of this improbable radar system is doubtful, but even without it, the lighthouse was an engineering marvel. It must have housed some sort of hydraulic machinery to haul up fuel for the nightly fires and control the moving figures. It must also have had a reflector, perhaps glass, perhaps polished metal, to carry the light of the blaze for so many miles.

Had the Alexandrians discovered the principle of the lens? It is possible, considering the abundance of mathematical scholars among them. Both Euclid and Aristarchus were alive in 297 B.C., when the lighthouse was built. But no one knows for sure. No diagrams have been found from that period, nor any descriptions. The best pictures came from engravings on old coins.

The big fire and the structure that housed it fell into the sea sometime in the eighth century A.D.; the circumstances are not known. The Arabs, who had been told that some of Alexander's vast treasure had been buried in the lighthouse, demolished some of the building itself. An earthquake wrecked the octagonal story in the twelfth century, and another finished off the first story, which fell into ruins. Thus the great lighthouse toppled, and finally one of the most remarkable structures ever constructed by man crumbled into dust. The lighthouse of Alexandria, along with the pyramids and the Colossus of Rhodes, is counted as one of the seven wonders of the ancient world. The minaret, the tower of a mosque from which Moslems are called to prayer, was often built on similar architectural lines, with the square base, octagonal middle, and circular top.

The great Alexandrian Library met the same sad fate of slow dismemberment. This time the destroyer was fire, or rather, a series of fires, although no one is sure. A great part of the library was undoubtedly burned during Caesar's siege of Alexandria in 47 B.C. But some of the volumes may have been saved, only to fall into the hands of other conquering invaders. Certainly not much of it was left when Alexandria was taken over by the Arabs in the seventh century A.D. There is a story about its final demise, whose terrible logic makes us wish to disprove it. When the precious books, parchments, and papyri were brought before the conquering caliph, Omar, he is reported to have said, "If these books agree with the Koran, they are unnecessary; if they disagree with the Koran, they are pernicious.   In either case, destroy them."

There is not much left to tell.   The last of the Ptolemies was Cleopatra, who inherited a lost cause.   By the time she ascended the throne at eighteen, Greece had sunk into a decline and the Roman empire was reaching formidable heights.   The late Ptolemies had become corrupt, debased, quarrelsome.   Her celebrated allure was undoubtedly a fact; her liaisons with Julius Caesar and Mark Antony have been much publicized, done to death in both fact and fiction.   She was certainly no dusky-haired vamp, as history often paints her.   Rather, she was cool-headed and ambitious, thinking in terms of her country as well as herself.   Her reddish-gold hair enhanced her female charm, and she used it, along with her astute brain, to try to gain her ends.   And what could those ends be, with such a powerful nation as Rome for her neighbor?   The best Cleopatra

Funeral masks were used in ancient days and became highly detailed over the years.   Museum of Cairo.

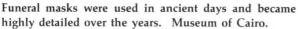

could hope for was a chance to rule her country under the shield of Roman power.

If Julius Caesar had lived, she might have saved a few shreds of dignity for Egypt.   But after his assassination there was little hope for friendly protection.   Cleopatra loved and bargained and fought—perhaps not too wisely or too well, but to the best of her ability.   When she directed her ships, with their purple sails, to put out to sea after the Battle of Actium in 31 B.C. and head for home, she knew she had lost Egypt to Octavius Caesar.

She died shortly after, at thirty-nine, probably by her own hand.   (Her last proud, defiant, pathetic words were later claimed to be: "I will *not* be led in *his* triumph.")   We can scarcely envision Cleopatra being led in shackles through the streets of Rome.   The story is that she had a servant woman smuggle a poisonous snake into her quarters.   Its sting produced a sure death, but not a disagreeable one.   (Had she considered the fitness of the symbol of the serpent—the royal cobra of Egypt?)

Her title of Cleopatra the Great marks her as a true queen, the noblest of all those Greeks who ruled Egypt after her illustrious predecessor—Alexander of Macedonia.

Thus Egypt's era of greatness came to a close, not quickly, but little by little, in a thousand ways, over a period of almost a thousand years.   Like the lighthouse, the library, the great buildings and statues, she simply tottered and crumbled into the sand.   We are reminded of Imperial China, first protected, then imprisoned, by her Great Wall.   Egypt's Great Wall was her geographical barriers, which for a time helped her to maintain her ironclad tradition but ultimately held her in a sort of vise.   Her inability to change in the face of great changes all around her contributed to her downfall.

Nevertheless, she maintained one of the longest continuous civilizations the world has ever known.   During more than half of all recorded history—from 3400 B.C. to A.D. 31—Egypt's name figures prominently, an important name among nations. Her feats of engineering, her eloquent art masterpieces, her great works produced with brush, string, knife, hammer and chisel have fortunately survived to make her remembered.

Egyptians were always busy. Look at any typical wall painting or bas relief in a tomb and you will see busy people coming to and fro—busy hunters in the marshes, busy sailors unloading ships, busy farmers tilling the soil. You will see busy scribes, builders, surveyors, all carrying on activities which make up the whole fabric of daily life. Look at the art of Sumer, or Babylonia, or Assyria, and you will see little of this. Battle scenes, dignified processions, solemn votaries, yes—but few clues as to how the ordinary man lived from day to day. The Egyptians had their battles and their processions too, and they memorialized them in their art. But the fact that they chose also to glorify the humdrum and the monotonous is the true key to their character.

Egypt's religious beliefs, naïve and tinged with magic, showed an effort to peer beyond the known into the unknown— not very far, perhaps, yet the solemn judgments of the dead indicated a dawning of conscience. Even more significant were the exhortations to live by the principles of Ma'at, the little seated goddess with the feather rising out of her headband, for whom no single abstract English word is adequate. Harmony, justice, balance—all are a part of Ma'at. Surely here is something which points to the two celebrated rules of the Greeks: "Nothing in excess" and "Know thyself," inscribed on the walls of the temple of Apollo at Delphi.

Centuries later, a Greek philosopher would lecture to his pupils about the tragic sterility of the "unexamined life," the life of a man who did not care where he had been and did not wonder where he was going. Egyptians did not worry about man's role in the vast scheme of things. (It remained for the Greeks to develop philosophy, or abstract speculation, to its greatest heights.) They knew what it was and accepted it.

They were true examiners of their lives in their own frame-work. Their concepts of right and wrong were searching and sharp. Although there were definite limitations to his thought, a man well knew his duty to his wife, his children, his servants, and his pharaoh. He reckoned each good day, each good crop, each year of generous flooding of the Nile as a gift of the god. What better reward could he have?

Perhaps the Egyptians' true reward lay in the ability to appreciate what they had. Perhaps they were truly blessed because they discovered the secret of accepting the gods' greatest gift, life itself, unmarred by the terrible compulsion to seek for more or to force their ideas on others.

Nations would come and go—more competitive, more ruthless, more articulate, perhaps more resilient. Glorious names would illuminate the pages of history, following Imhotep, Hatshepsut, Akhenaton, Ramses. But Egypt would remain the first custodian of man's ancient birthright: to love and be loved; to live and let live.

To the world Egypt also left specific legacies. The calendar fills man's first need to observe, to measure time, and to live with nature. The science of medicine is a constant challenge to acquire knowledge for the betterment of the human condition and the relief of suffering. But it is the art of writing which makes it possible for every human being to communicate with his fellows. Egyptians were not the first to learn how to write, but they were unquestionably the first to use writing in such a way that one mind could reach out and touch another. The first picture-symbols of birds, animals, and the familiars of everyday living could convey love. They could comfort. They could instruct. They could entertain.

The gift of shared emotion, or shared experience, was a priceless legacy to the civilizations that were to rise and fall and rise again in the Western World.

Suggested Reading

Aldred, Cyril. *Egypt to the End of the Old Kingdom.* Thames and Hudson, London, 1965. *The Development of Ancient Egypt, 3200-1315.* Taranti, London, 1952. Detailed histories of the periods.

Book of the Dead. Transcript of Ani, the translation into English and an introduction by E. A. Wallis Budge. University Books, 1960. Scholarly treatment. The many pages of clear hieroglyphic script are well worth examining.

Cambridge Ancient History. Revised edition of Volumes I-II. Cambridge University Press, Cambridge, England, 1962. Pamphlets written by eminent scholars.

Desroches-Noblecourt, Christiane. *The World Saves Abu Simbel.* Verlag A. F. Koska, Vienna. Art volume with dramatic color photos and detailed text.

Desroches-Noblecourt, Christiane. *Tutankhamen—Life and Death of a Pharaoh.* New York Graphic Society, 1963. Art volume. Handsome illustrations in color.

Edwards, I. E. S. *The Pyramids of Egypt.* Parish, London, 1961. The pyramids, their meaning and significance.

Erman, Adolph. *The Ancient Egyptians.* Harper Torch Book (1233 T), New York, 1965. Brief, readable history.

Frankfurt, Henri. *Ancient Egyptian Religion—An Interpretation.* Harper Torch Book (TB 77), New York, 1965. One of various interpretations of Egyptian religious belief.

Frazer, Sir James George. *Golden Bough.* One vol. Macmillan. 1958. Condensed edition of well known classic offers insights into the complexities of Egyptian mythology and culture.

Gardiner, A. *Egyptian Grammar: Being an Introduction to the Study of Hieroglyphics.* Third Edition Revised. Oxford University Press, Oxford, England, 1966. For those who wish to pursue further the study of hieroglyphics.

Hayes, William Charles. *The Scepter of Egypt.* Two vols. Metropolitan Museum, New York, 1959. Guide to the Egyptian Collection of the Metropolitan Museum of Art expanded to include useful detail on art, culture, and religion.

Herodotus. *The Persian Wars.* Chapter II. Modern Library. Lively, first-hand report of Egypt in 470 B.C. Recommended to all students of ancient history.

Keese, Hermann. *Ancient Egypt—A Cultural Topography.* Faber and Faber, London, 1961. A detailed study of the climate and geography of ancient Egypt, area by area.

Lange, Kurt, and Max Hirmer. *3,000 Years of Egyptian Art and Architecture.* Speiden, New York, 1968. Excellent reproductions of Egyptian art works.

Lucas, Alfred. *Ancient Egyptian Materials and Industries.* Fourth Edition, revised and enlarged by John Richard Harris. St. Martin's, New York, 1962. Interesting detail on the material accomplishments of the Egyptians.

Mekhitarian, Arpag. *Egyptian Painting.* Albert Skira, Geneva, 1954. Art volume. Superb color reproductions and informative text.

Posener, George, ed. *Dictionary of Egyptian Civilization.* Tudor, New York, 1959. Handy reference text.

Smith, William Stevenson. *Ancient Egypt—A General History of Egyptian Art.* (Paperback.) Beacon Press for Boston Museum of Fine Arts, Boston, 1960. A short description of the development of Egyptian art.

Index